CAESAR

INVASION of BRITAIN

Bust of Julius Caesar

CAESAR
INVASION
of BRITAIN

Text ✦ Notes ✦ Exercises ✦ Vocabulary ✦ Illustrations

W. Welch ✦ C. G. Duffield

Bolchazy-Carducci Publishers, Inc.
Wauconda, Illinois
by arrangement with Macmillan Education Ltd.

Cover design:
Charlene Hernandez

First Published by Macmillan Education Ltd., 1884
© Macmillan Education Ltd.

Bolchazy-Carducci Publishers, Inc.
1000 Brown Street, Unit 101
Wauconda, IL 60084 USA

http://www.bolchazy.com

ISBN: 0-86516-334-0

Printed in the United States of America
2000
by Bang Printing

FOREWORD

Caesar's *De Bello Gallico* enjoyed pride of place in the traditional Latin curriculum. The student's first task in translation (after mastering Latin grammar) was usually a slow and painstaking reading of Caesar, concentrating in great detail on the syntax of Caesar's Latin, often to the exclusion of his narrative. In the mid-twentieth century a reaction set in which unjustifiably rejected Caesar as "boring" and "unable to stimulate student interest." This prejudice probably reveals more about the methods used in the classroom than it does about the material, for there is no reason that Caesar should be thought "boring": his story moves rapidly and is told with consummate skill; the clarity of his style is proverbial and provides the best possible model for the student just starting to read Latin. On both counts, Caesar deserves to be reinstated in the standard Latin curriculum in colleges and high schools.

One of the most exciting episodes in the whole Gallic campaign was the invasion of Britain by the Roman army for the first time. Caesar's first attempt, in 55 B.C., was a near-disaster, but his second (the following year) was a military success that took the Roman standards from the coast of Kent as far inland as the River Thames and beyond. In books IV and V of the *De Bello Gallico,* Caesar provides a vivid and exciting account of these two campaigns that will certainly catch the interest of most students. It is presented in clear and flowing Latin, and the combination of readable Latin and an exciting tale (important to the history not only of Rome but of England as well) makes the British expedition particularly suitable for Latin students who have had the basic introductory sequence of courses.

This text, *The Invasion of Britain,* was adapted from Caesar's original by Welch and Duffield with just such students in mind. At first the Latin is simplified, but the students' skills are carefully nurtured by the passages until they are reading Caesar's Latin practically undiluted. Furthermore, the book provides illustrations, maps, notes, vocabulary, and composition exercises based on the passages, all of which enrich both its historical and paedagogical utility. Caesar should be returned to the Latin classroom as a model of style for students learning the language, and the reprinting of this excellent graded reader is an important step in that direction. As a university Latin teacher, I use the book in my own classes, and can warmly endorse its adoption by others.

Prof. James C. Anderson
The University of Georgia

CONTENTS

LIST OF ILLUSTRATIONS

The portrait, which has suffered from cleaning, but is undoubtedly ancient, represents Caesar in old age; he is inclined to baldness, and his cheeks are shrunken. We know that he is said to have worn a wreath to hide his baldness; and Suetonius also says that for the same purpose he combed his scanty hair forward, as we see it represented on this head.

Julius Caesar, who is described as CAESAR DICT(ator) PERPETUO, is represented wearing a thick laurel wreath. This is one of the latest portraits executed during the Dictator's lifetime.

The types of this coin are, though it may seem incredible, merely a degradation of the types of the gold stater of Philip II. of Macedon. On the obverse, the remains of the laurel-wreath are visible; on the reverse the horse is practically all that remains of the two horses and chariot with charioteer. The rest is meaningless ornament invented by the fancy of the barbarian out of a type which, as it became more and more degraded by unintelligent copying, he more and more failed to understand.

Caesar (*Bell. Gall.* v. 12) says of the Britons: 'Utuntur aut aere aut nummo aureo aut taleis ferreis ad certum pondus examinatis pro nummo.' Since we have gold coins of the Britons dating back to a period long before Caesar's invasion—these coins can hardly be later than 100 B.C.—there is no reason for bracketing as spurious the words 'aut nummo aureo,' as some editors do. The words which should be bracketed are 'aut aere' ; they have probably come in from the statement made below: 'aere utuntur importato.'

Relief from Pompeii.

The details of this *navis oneraria* are very clear. The aplustre ends in a goose-head (χηνίσκος), to which is fastened a flagstaff (στυλίς) with ensign. The steersman (*gubernator*) controls the steering-oar (*gubernaculum*). The crew are engaged in furling (*contrahere*) the sails; one of them is running up the shrouds, another is on the fore-stay; two are on the yard (*antenna*), which is spliced. An ensign also flies from the masthead. The figure-head is a head of Minerva or Roma in a helmet.

From a grave-stone at Bonn, of the first century after Christ.
The ground is imaginary.

Pintaius the *signifer,* from whose grave-stone this illustration is taken, wears over his head and shoulders a skin, which covers the helmet of which the checkpieces are visible. Under his jerkin is a coat of mail (*lorica*), and under that a *tunica*. On his feet are toeless boots. He wears sword and dagger in belts which gird his waist. The *signum* is decorated with (beginning from the top) a wreath, cross-bar with pendants, metal disc, the eagle of Jupiter standing on a thunderbolt, crescent moon, etc.

From a relief in the Louvre, about the beginning of the
Christian era. The ground is imaginary.

The soldiers wear coats of mail (*lorica hamata*), not scale-armour, as suggested in the illustration, over their tunics, and carry short daggers. The shield of the one on the left has for device a winged thunderbolt.

From a relief at Verona of Imperial date.
The ground is imaginary.

This is the grave-stone of Q. Sertorius, a centurion of the Eleventh Legion, known as the 'Claudia pia fidelis.' He carries the wand (*vitis*) of office, and wears the *corona civica* of oak-leaves (little but the tie of this crown is visible in the illustration). Over his tunica he wears a coat of scale-armour (*lorica squamata*); his phalerae are fastened on the usual framework, and two *torques* hang from his neck. The circular object by his left hand is the pommel of his sword. He also wears greaves (*ocreae*) and boots (*caligae*), and carries his cloak (*sagum*).

This is the grave-stone of one C. Marius. The deceased is armed with a six-sided shield and spear. The metal discs on the frame which covers his breast are *phalerae*, decorations (*dona militaria*) more or less corresponding to our war medals; we see them again on a larger scale at the bottom of the relief. The two bracelets represented at the side of the *phalerae* and the two pairs of *torques* above the niche are further decorations.

This figure-head may possibly have belonged to one of the smaller vessels engaged in the battle of Actium (31 B.C.).It is known that Augustus owed his success to the small *naves Liburnae*. The bust represents the goddess Roma,wearing a helmet and aegis.

The galley is proceeding to the right. The stern carries an aplustre and small circular shield (not well shown on this specimen); the stem runs up in the form usual at this time. There are small cabins in the forecastle and poop; from the former rises a foremast carrying a pennon (?). The inscription is ANT. AVG. III. VIR. R. P. C., *i.e.* 'Antonius augur triumvir reipublicae constituendae.' On the reverse is an an *aquila* between two *signa* ornamented with discs. The inscription is CHORTIVM PRAETORIARVM, showing that the coin was struck for the payment of the Praetorian Cohorts, or Guards. Note the form CHORTIVM, which is not uncommon in Latin inscriptions.

From a relief on Trajan's Column, 113 A.D.

This figure represents one of a party engaged in storming Sarmizegetusa, the Dacian capital. He holds the sling, with the bolt in it, in his right hand. The sling is a short one, and the left hand is apparently not used in discharging it.

*From a relief on the Column of Marcus Aurelius
(shortly after 169 A.D.).*

This represents an attack on a German fortress, the wall of which seems to be made of wattles. The Romans approach *testudine facta, i.e.* placing their shields close together and overlapping so that missiles glide off, as they would off the back of a tortoise. Torches, swords, a pot full of molten metal, stones, spears, etc., are the missiles used by the defenders.

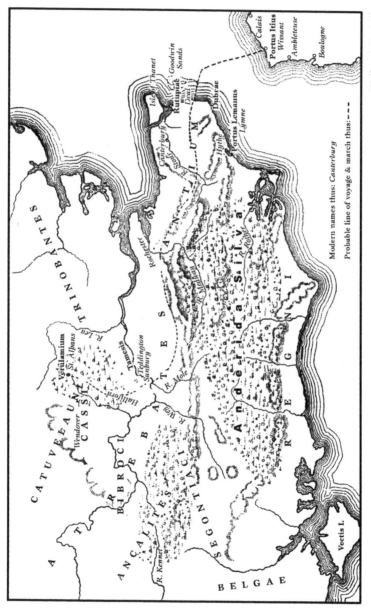

MAP FOR THE INVASION OF BRITAIN

Walker & Boutall

Modern names thus: *Canterbury*

Probable line of voyage & march thus: – – –

INTRODUCTION

Julius Caesar in Britain

THE transactions recorded in this book should be of the highest importance to Englishmen, for, however transient in their effects, they mark the dawn of the history of our island. Before the year 55 B.C., Britain was a *terra incognita* to the ancient world at Rome. The first mention of the island by any Roman writer is found only in the second book of Caesar's Gallic War, and even then he knew next to nothing about it. In 55 B.C. all Gaul lay prostrate at the feet of the conqueror; one by one the tribes had succumbed, and although they were only waiting an opportunity to strike again for freedom, the advancing legions had carried their victorious arms to the northern sea-coast of Gaul. Suddenly a new danger arose; the barbarous hordes of Germany poured across the Rhine upon their helpless neighbours; Caesar was summoned hastily from Rome and hurrying across the wintry passes of the Alps he met the invader near the junction of the Mosa and the

Rhenus, and after a most determined battle nearly anni-
hilated two entire tribes. It was at this time that the
invasion of Britain was determined upon. If Gaul were
to be preserved as a Roman dependency, it must be
delivered from foreign foe and foreign ally alike. A
severe example had just been made of one of the former, which would intimidate the rest for some time to
come. But this was not enough. Caesar reflected that,
in the conflict with the Veneti the year before, when
all the maritime tribes had sent help against him, a fleet
had sailed in from the direction of the white cliffs that
lay far out on the horizon, and had joined the Venetian
League. This was enough. If the security of his Gallic
conquests was to be preserved, this mysterious ally from
across the sea must be taught the power of the Roman
arms. An unconquered people, so close at hand, would
offer an example of independence highly dangerous to
the peace of Gaul. At all hazards, therefore, the Britons
must be silenced. Caesar took up his quarters on the
coast of the Morini, who provided him with information and assistance. Volusenus, a Roman officer, was
sent to reconnoitre the opposite coast. Commius, chief
of the Atrebates, was commissioned to precede the
Romans and impress upon the Britons the advisability
of an alliance or submission to the Roman power. The
autumn was advancing; little way could be made this
year, an expedition would not be thrown away however, and so upon the evening of the 26th of August,

B.C. 55, two divisions, consisting of two legions and a few hundred cavalry, were arranged to sail from two ports in the country of the Morini. Caesar with his legions made a favourable passage, and in a few hours was under the Dover cliffs where the hostile tribesmen were gathered to repel the invader. To land here was impracticable, and the other squadron of ships had not yet arrived. Accordingly Caesar drifted up seven or eight miles with the tide and arrived off the flat beach of Deal. The Britons were on the alert, and rushed into the waves to bar his landing. A hard fight followed; the Britons fought stubbornly; the ships of war drawn up on the flanks poured volley after volley of darts upon them; the Britons were dazed but unbeaten, when an ensign of the 10th legion, calling on his comrades to follow, dashed into the water at their head and drove back the Britons upon the shore. Their courage failed and they fled. A fortified camp was constructed on the shore, and the Britons at once began to send embassies with overtures of peace. Meantime Caesar's other detachment had been less fortunate; detained in harbour for four days after the first had sailed, they started at last to join the main body of ships. They were no sooner sighted from the camp on shore than a strong gale sprang up from the east and beat them down channel; some succeeded, however, in making the coast of Gaul in safety, while others were driven down the coast of Britain. This storm nearly proved fatal to the Romans

on shore. The war vessels drawn upon the beach were
shattered by the breakers, the transports at anchor were
dragged from their moorings and dashed upon the coast.
Nor was this the only misadventure. About the same
time the Britons made an attack upon the seventh
legion, which had been sent upon a foraging expedition, but as it was not out of communication with the
camp, they were repulsed. Not a moment was to be
lost. The shattered vessels were repaired, and in view
of the coming stormy season, offers of submission made
by the barbarians were accepted, and Caesar set sail for
Gaul without delay.

In the spring of B.C. 54, preparations were completed
for a descent upon Britain with a much larger force.
Six hundred transports, with five legions and the pick
of the Gallic cavalry on board, sailed from Portus Itius
and, without casualty, landed at the same spot as in
the preceding summer. A naval station was constructed on the shore, and a permanent camp pitched at some
distance inland without the slightest opposition. It was
not until he arrived at the banks of the little river Stour
that he met with any bar to his progress, and even then
the Britons at once fell back upon their entrenchment,
a clearing in a neighbouring wood, where they were
dislodged by the seventh legion. Next day news came
from Q. Atrius, who had been left behind on shore to
guard the naval station, that a storm on the previous
night had again wrought havoc amongst the fleet. To

prevent similar destruction for the future, Caesar determined to beach the remainder of the fleet and fortify
the vessels with a camp on the shore, a task costing his
men ten days of ceaseless labour. Meanwhile the British
tribes had rallied under Cassivellaunus, a chief of the
Catuvelauni, and were prepared to dispute his advance
at the river Stour. The fleet secured, Caesar rejoined
his legions, and a most determined battle ensued. Again
and again the Britons in their war-chariots dashed at
the Roman lines, but they never gave way, while the
former lost the flower of their warriors. The Roman
arms won the day, and never again was Caesar met in
the open field. In spite of numerous irregular skirmishes
he pushed on boldly, and arrived at the banks of the
Thames, at a spot eighty miles from the sea. Here he
found a ford, but the opposite bank was fortified with
stakes driven into it, and the enemy were waiting to
receive him. It is almost impossible to say where this
spot was, but a long cherished tradition has fixed upon
Cowey Stakes – an old ford on the river near the junction of the Wey with the Thames – as the place where
Caesar crossed. No real opposition was encountered
here, the Romans forded the river easily, carrying all
before them, and Caesar marched straight on
Verulamium, the stronghold of Cassivellaunus. On his
way he received the submission of the Trinobantes,
over whom Cassivellaunus had usurped authority, as
well as that of several other tribes, and Cassivellaunus

had to meet the invaders with only a handful of fol-
lowers sheltered in the morasses and thickets in which
his capital lay. Here he held out for a time; he urged
the Britons of Cantium to attack the Roman camp on
the shore, which they did without success. His last
chance was gone, and he surrendered to the Romans
on hearing of the failure of the attack.

Caesar was now in haste to return to Gaul. News
had reached him that a spirit of rebellion was abroad
there, and to quell it his legions must return. After
exacting tribute and hostages from Cassivellaunus he
re-embarked his legions and sailed away to Gaul, never
to return. Thus ended a most fruitless expedition. The
Britons were beaten, yet no territory was added to the
Roman power; not a single garrison was left behind;
no British wealth was poured into the treasury at Rome;
no train of captive Britons trod the Sacra Via before
the conqueror's chariot. Much bravery and determina-
tion, many lives, and a large number of vessels had
been thrown away upon it with this result. As Tacitus
says in his 'Agricola,' Caesar "rather showed Britain to
posterity than handed it down to them as a conquest."
It was not until nearly a hundred years later, in the
reign of the Emperor Claudius (A.D. 43 and 44), that
any part of Britain was annexed to the Roman empire.

(The localities mentioned above are disputed by var-
ious writers; many places contend for the honour of
Caesar's landing-place, but the views of Mr. George Long

Contemporary British Coin. From the British Museum

Portrait of Julius Caesar on a Coin of Buca

Navis Oneraria (Schreiber-Anderson.)

Type Etching Co.

on such matters have been adopted, and to him the editors are indebted for help in other parts of the book.)

DIRECTIONS FOR TRANSLATING

1. Pick out the finite verb (the **predicate**) and find out its voice, mood, tense, number, and person.

2. Find the **subject** or subjects with which it agrees. Translate.

3. If the verb is incomplete, find the **object** or **completion**. Translate.

4. See if the **subject** is **enlarged** by any of the methods mentioned below; if it is, translate, taking the **enlargements** with the subject.

5. See if the **object** is **enlarged**, if it is, translate, taking the **enlargements** with the object.

6. Take the **extensions of the predicate**. Translate.

7. Translate finally, putting in the introductory conjunctions or other words not yet taken.

The **subject** may be
1. A noun.
2. A pronoun (perhaps understood in the verb).
3. An adjective.
4. An infinitive mood.
5. A phrase.

The **subject** may be **enlarged** by
1. An adjective or participle.
2. An noun in apposition.
3. A noun in the genitive case.
4. A relative clause.
5. A participial phrase.

The **object** or **completion** may consist of a phrase or of any of the parts of speech which can form a **subject**.

The **object** may be enlarged in the same way as the **subject**.

The **predicate** may be extended by
1. Adverb.
2. Ablative case.
3. Preposition and its case.
4. Adverbial sentence.

RULES OF AGREEMENT

1. The verb agrees with its subject in number and person (and gender in the compound tenses).

2. The adjective agrees with its substantive in gender, number, and case.

3. The relative agrees with its antecedent in gender and number; for case it looks to its own verb.

PARSING

1. *Verb.* Person, number, tense, mood, and voice, from _____ (give the parts). Agrees with _____, its subject.

2. *Noun.* Case, number, and gender, from _____, of the _____ declension. Give the reason for the case.

3. *Adjective.* Case, number, and gender, from _____ and is declined like _____. It agrees with its substantive _____. Give the comparative and superlative.

4. *Relative.* Case, number, and gender, from _____. It agrees with its antecedent _____. Give the reason for the case.

ROMAN STANDARD-BEARER
From a Gravestone at Bonn; of the First Century A.D.

ROMAN LEGIONARIES
From a Relief in the Louvre;
about the beginning of the Christian Era

ROMAN CENTURION

From a Relief at Verona of Imperial Date

CAESAR'S INVASION OF BRITAIN

1. Jam exigua pars aestatis reliqua fuit:

Caesar tamen in Britanniam profi- Caesar makes inquiries
cisci statuit:

Britanni in omnibus fere Gallicis bellis auxilium
hostibus nostris subministraverant.   5

2. Sed primò genus hominum, loca, portus, aditus
cognoscere statuit:

haec omnia fere Gallis erant incognita.

Nemo enim, praeter mercatores, illò adiit:

neque iis ipsis quidquam praeter oram maritimam   10
notum est.

3. Itaque mercatores ad se convocat.

Sed ea quae maxime cognoscere volebat, insulae
magnitudinem, incolarum genus, usum belli, reperire
non poterat.   15

C. Volusenum cum navi longâ praemittit:

ipse autem cum omnibus suis copiis   His preparations.
in Morinos proficiscitur:

inde erat brevissimus in Britanniam trajectus.

4. Huc naves undique venire jubet: 20 et classem, quam ad Veneticum bellum effecerat, convenire jubet.

Interim consilium ejus per mercatores ad Britannos perlatum est:

25   legati ab insulae civitatibus ad eum veniunt:

obsides dare et imperio populi Romani obtemperare volunt.

5. Caesar, liberaliter pollicitus, eos domum remittit. Commium autem unà cum iis mittit:

30   hunc Caesar regem constituerat:

hujus virtutem et consilium probabat:

Commius enim Caesari fidelis esse videbatur:

et ejus auctoritas in his regionibus magna habebatur.

Volusenus autem neque e navi egredi neque se

35 barbaris committere audet.

Itaque quinto die ad Caesarem redit:

et, quae viderit, renuntiat.

Help given him by the Morini.   6. Caesar in his locis moratur: et naves parat:

40   Legati ex magnâ parte Morinorum ad eum veniunt:

de superioris temporis consilio se excusant:

olim enim bellum populo Romano fecerant.

Hoc Caesari esse opportunum videbatur:

nam neque post tergum hostem relinquere volebat,

45   neque facultatem belli gerendi propter anni tempus habebat.

His magnum numerum obsidum imperat, et eos in fidem recipit.

Trooper (Schreiber-Anderson)

Figure-head of Galley.
From original in the British Museum.

Warship and Standards. Coin of M. Antonius.

7. Naves circiter octoginta onerarias cogit:
hae satis esse numero ei videbantur: 50
sed praeter eas quasdam naves longas habebat:
has quaestori, legatis praefectisque distribuit.
Huc accedebant duodeviginti onerariae naves,
    quae ex eo loco ab millibus passuum octo vento
tenebantur: 55
    has equitibus distribuit.
    Publium Sulpicium Rufum legatum cum praesidio
portum tenere jussit.
    8. Mox tempestatem ad navigationem idoneam
nactus est: 60
    tum naves tertiâ fere vigiliâ solvit:
    equitesque in ulteriorem portum progredi, et naves
conscendere, et se sequi jussit.
    Ipse autem horâ circiter diei quartâ cum primis
navibus Britanniam attigit: 65
    et ibi armatas hostium copias in omnibus collibus
expositas conspexit.
    9. Haec erat loci natura:
    mare angustis montibus continebatur:
    telum ex locis superioribus in litus adigi pote-   70
rat.
    Hic nequaquam idoneus locus esse videbatur:
    et ad nonam horam reliquas naves in ancoris
exspectabat.
    Interim legatos tribunosque militum convocat, et eos 75
hortatur.

Postea et ventum et aestum uno tempore secundum
nanciscitur:

signum dedit: ancorae sublatae sunt.

80   10. Tum circiter millia passuum septem ab eo loco
progressus est,

et naves in aperto ac plano litore constituit.

At barbari consilium Romanorum cognoscunt:

The Britons show   equitatum et essedarios praemittunt:
fight.
85   hoc plerumque genere militiae in
proeliis uti consuescunt.

Itaque subsecuti reliquis copiis nostros e navibus
egredi prohibent.

11. Erat ob has causas summa difficultas:

90   naves propter magnitudinem nisi in alto constitui
non poterant:

militibus nostris loca ignota erant:

manus eorum impeditae erant:

ipsi magno et gravi onere armorum oppressi erant.

95   Hostes autem aut ex arido, aut paulum in aquam
progressi, audacter tela conjecerunt:

et equos insuefactos incitaverunt.

12. Quibus rebus nostri perterriti, atque hujus omnino
generis pugnae imperiti, non solitâ alacritate utebantur.

100 The Britons receive   Quod ubi Caesar animadvertit, naves
a check. Pluck of a
Roman standard- longas paulum removeri ab onerariis
bearer.
navibus, et remis incitari, et ad
latus apertum hostium constitui, atque inde fundis,
sagittis, tormentis hostes propelli ac summoveri jus-

sit: (navium longarum et species erat barbaris inusi- 105
tatior et motus ad usum expeditior).

Quae res magno usui nostris fuit.

Nam barbari, et navium figurâ et remorum motu
et inusitato genere tormentorum permoti, constiterunt
ac paulum modo pedem rettulerunt.   110

13. Atque nostris militibus cunctantibus, maxime
propter altitudinem maris, quidam decimae legionis
aquilifer, contestatus deos, ut ea res legioni feliciter
eveniret: *"Desilīte,"* inquit, *"milites, nisi vultis aquilam
hostibus prodere: ego certe meum reipublicae atque imperatori* 115
officium praestitero." Mox se ex navi projecit atque in
hostes aquilam ferre coepit. Tum nostri, tantum
dedecus metuentes, universi ex navi desiluerunt. Hos
item ex proximis navibus ubi conspexerant, subsecuti
hostibus adpropinquârunt.   120

14. Pugnatum est ab utrisque acriter. Nostri tamen
magnopere perturbabantur: nam ne-   Engagement on the
que ordines servare neque firmiter in-   beach. Victory of the
                                         Romans.
sistere, neque signa subsequi poterant, atque alius aliâ
ex navi, quibuscumque signis occurrerat, se aggrega- 125
bat. Hostes vero, notis omnibus vadis, ubi ex litore
aliquos singulares ex navi egredientes conspexerant,
equos incitabant: nostros impeditos adoriebantur:
plures paucos circumsistebant: alii ab latere aperto in
universos tela conjiciebant. 15. Quod ubi viderat 130
Caesar, scaphas longarum navium, item speculatoria
navigia a militibus compleri jussit, et iis, quos laborantes

conspexerat, subsidia submittebat. Nostri ubi in
arido constiterunt, suis omnibus consecutis, in hostes
135 impetum fecerunt atque eos in fugam dederunt: neque
longius prosequi potuerunt, quod equites cursum
tenere atque insulam capere non potuerant. Hoc unum ad
pristinam fortunam Caesari defuit.

    16. Hostes, proelio superati, simul atque se ex fugâ
140 receperunt, statim ad Caesarem legatos
de pace miserunt: promittunt se obsides daturos esse, et Caesaris mandata
effecturos. Unà cum his legatis Commius Atrebas
venit, qui a Caesare in Britanniam antea praemissus
145 erat. Hunc Britanni, e navi egressum, quum ad eos
oratoris modo Caesaris mandata deferret, comprehend-
erant atque in vincula conjecerant. 17. Tum proelio
facto, remiserunt et ejus rei culpam in multitudinem
contulerunt, et ut ignosceretur propter imprudentiam
150 petiverunt. Caesar questus est, quod bellum sine causâ
intulissent; dixit se ignoscere imprudentiae obsidesque
imperavit: quorum illi partem statim dederunt, partem ex longinquioribus locis arcessitam se daturos
paucis diebus dixerunt. Interea suos remigrare in
155 agros jusserunt, principesque undique convenire, et se
civitatesque suas Caesari commendare coeperunt.

    18. Pace confirmatâ, naves duode-
viginti, quae equites sustulerant ex
superiore portu leni vento solverunt. Quae quum
160 appropinquarent Britanniae et ex castris viderentur

The Britons sue for peace and restore Commius, the envoy, whom they held in custody.

Destruction of the Roman fleet by a storm.

magna tempestas subitò coorta est: neque ulla navis cursum tenere poterat; sed aliae eodem, unde erant profectae, referebantur, aliae ad inferiorem partem insulae, quae est propius solis occasum, magno sui cum periculo dejiciebantur: quae tamen, ancoris jactis, 165 fluctibus complebantur: itaque necessariò adversâ nocte in altum provectae continentem petiverunt. Eâdem nocte accidit, ut esset luna plena, qui dies maritimos aestus maximos in Oceano efficere consuevit; nostrisque id erat incognitum. 19. Ita uno tempore et 170 longas naves, quibus Caesar exercitum transportaverat, quasque in aridum subduxerat, aestus complebat, et onerarias, quae ad ancoras erant deligatae, tempestas afflictabat; neque ulla nostris facultas aut administrandi aut auxiliandi dabatur. Complures naves 175 fractae sunt; reliquae, funibus, ancoris, reliquisque armamentis amissis, erant ad navigandum inutiles: itaque magna totius exercitûs perturbatio facta est. Neque enim naves erant aliae, quibus reportari possent, et omnia, quibus naves refici possent, deerant: et 180 quòd Caesaris consilium hiemandi in Galliâ omnibus cognitum est, frumentum his in locis in hiemem non provisum erat.

20. Quibus rebus cognitis, principes Britanniae, qui post proelium ad Caesarem convene- Overjoyed at Ro- 185
man misfortunes
rant inter se colloquuntur. Romanis the Britons renew
hostilities.
deesse equites et naves et frumentum in-
telligunt; et paucitatem militum ex castrorum exi-

guitate cognoscunt: quae castra hoc erant etiam angus-
190 tiora, quod sine impedimentis Caesar legiones transportaverat. Constituunt, rebellione factâ, nostros frumento
commeatuque prohibere, et rem in hiemem producere;
his superatis aut reditu interclusis, neminem postea in
Britanniam transiturum belli inferendi causâ confidunt.
195 Itaque rursus conjuratione factâ, paulatim ex castris
discedere, ac suos clam ex agris deducere coeperunt.

    21. Caesar nondum eorum consilia cognoverat:
Caesar repairs the tamen et ex eventu navium suarum et
shattered fleet.
ex eo, quod obsides dare intermiserant,
200 fore id, quod accidit, suspicabatur. Itaque ad omnes
casus subsidia comparabat. Nam et frumentum ex agris
quotidie in castra conferebat, et materiâ atque aere earum navium, quae gravissime afflictae erant, ad reliquas
reficiendas utebatur; alia, quae ad eas res usui erant, ex
205 continenti comportari jubebat. Quae res summo studio
a militibus administrabatur: itaque, duodecim navibus
amissis, reliquis ut navigare commode posset, effecit.

    22. Dum ea geruntur, una legio, quae appellabatur
The Romans sur- septima, ex consuetudine frumentatum
prised by an ambus-
210 cade of the Britons. missa est: nulla ad id tempus suspicio
belli interposita erat: pars hominum in agris remanebat,
pars etiam in castra ventitabat: ii, qui pro portis
castrorum in statione erant, Caesari nuntiaverunt pul-
verem magnum atque inusitatum in eâ parte videri,
215 quam in partem legio iter fecisset. Caesar aliquid novi
consilii a barbaris initum esse suspicabatur. Itaque

cohortes, quae in stationibus erant, secum in eam partem proficisci jussit: duas ex reliquis cohortes in stationem succedere, reliquas armari et confestim sese subsequi jussit. 23. Quum paulo longius a castris pro- 220 cessisset, suos ab hostibus premi animadvertit: con- fertâ legione, ex omnibus partibus tela conjiciebantur. Nam omni frumento ex reliquis partibus demesso, pars una erat reliqua: hostes suspicati nostros huc esse venturos noctu in silvis delituerant: tum subitò 225 nostros dispersos adoriuntur: nam illi, occupati in metendo, arma deposuerant: itaque, paucis interfectis, reliquos incertis ordinibus perturbant: simul equitatu atque essedis nostros circumdant.

24. Genus hoc est ex essedis pugnae. Primo per 230 omnes partes perequitant, et tela conji- British mode of fighting. Their use ciunt: ipso terrore equorum et strepitu of chariots. rotarum ordines plerumque perturbantur: tum quum se inter turmas equitum insinuaverunt, ex essedis desili- unt, et pedibus proeliantur. Aurigae interim paulatim 235 ex proelio excedunt: atque ita currus collocant ut, si essedarii a multitudine hostium premantur, expedi- tum ad suos receptum habeant. 25. Ita mobilitatem equitum, stabilitatem peditum in proeliis praestant: ac tantum usu et quotidianâ exercitatione efficiunt, ut 240 in declivi ac praecipiti loco incitatos equos sustinere possint: et brevi spatio eos moderari ac flectere, et per temonem percurrere, et in jugo insistere, et se inde in currus citissime recipere solent.

Nostri milites novitate pugnae perturbantur: quibus
245 tempore opportunissimo Caesar auxilium tulit: namque ejus adventu
hostes constiterunt, nostri se ex timore
receperunt. 26. Sed Caesar alienum
esse tempus ad committendum proe-
250 lium arbitrabatur: ita suo se loco continuit, et post
aliquid temporis in castra legiones reduxit. Dum haec
geruntur, nostri omnes occupati sunt: reliqui, qui
erant in agris, discesserunt. Tempestates continuos
complures dies secutae sunt: quae et nostros in castris
255 continebant, et hostem a pugnâ prohibebant. Interim
barbari nuntios in omnes partes dimiserunt, paucita-
temque nostrorum militum suis praedicaverunt: et
demonstraverunt, quanta daretur facultas praedae
faciendae ac libertatis occupandae, si Romanos castris
260 expulissent. Itaque, magnâ multitudine peditatûs
equitatûsque coactâ, ad castra venerunt.

27. Caesar autem animadvertit hostes, si pellerentur,
celeritate periculum effugere posse:
quae res superioribus diebus acciderat.
Itaque nactus equites circiter triginta
265 quos Commius Atrebas secum transportaverat, legiones
in acie pro castris constituit. Hostes, commisso proelio, diutius impetum nostrorum militum ferre non
potuerunt, ac terga verterunt. Quos nostri spatio
270 brevi secuti sunt: complures ex iis occiderunt; deinde,
omnibus longe lateque aedificiis incensis, se in castra

Caesar's arrival on the scene stops the battle. Taking advantage of the delay caused by storms, the Britons increase their forces for a fresh attack.

The Roman camp attacked. The Britons routed and pursued with slaughter.

receperunt. Eodem die legati ab hostibus missi ad Caesarem de pace venerunt. 28. His Caesar nume- rum obsidum, quem antea imperaverat, The Britains surren- der and Caesar duplicavit: eosque in continentem ad- returns to Gaul. 275 duci jussit. Ipse, idoneam tempestatem nactus, paulo post mediam noctem naves solvit: quae omnes incolu- mes ad continentem pervenerunt: sed ex iis onerariae duae portus capere non potuerunt, et paulo infra delatae sunt. 280

Caesar in Belgis omnium legionum hiberna constituit. Eò duae civitates ex Britanniâ obsides Preparations made du- ring the winter for a sec- miserunt, reliquae neglexerunt. Ro- ond invasion to be undertaken in the fol- mae ex litteris Caesaris dierum viginti lowing summer. supplicatio a senatu decreta est. Interim naves aedifi- 285 cari veteresque refici jubet: ipse in fines Trevirorum profectus est, quod hi neque ad concilia veniebant neque imperio parebant. 29. Inde ad portum Itium pervenit, quò naves convenire jusserat, quòd inde erat brevissimus in Britanniam trajectus. Dies circiter 290 viginti quinque in eo loco commoratus est, quòd Corus ventus navigationem impediebat, qui mag- nam partem omnis temporis his in locis flare con- suevit. Tandem idoneam nactus tempestatem milites equitesque conscendere in naves jubet. Labienum in 295 continente cum tribus legionibus et millibus duobus equitum relinquit, ut portus tueatur et frumentum provideat. Ipse cum quinque legionibus et pari numero equitum, quem in continente reliquerat, ad

300 solis occasum naves solvit. 30. Primo leni Africo

The fleet crosses the provectus est: mox tamen mediâ cir-
Channel. Its appearance
strikes terror into the citer nocte, vento intermisso, cursum
Britons.
    non tenuit et aestu longius delatus

est: ortâ luce sub sinistra Britanniam relictam con-

305 spexit. Tum rursus aestus commutationem secutus

remis contendit, ut eam partem insulae caperet, quâ

optimus esset egressus. Quâ in re militum virtus

admodum fuit laudanda; qui vectoriis gravibusque

navigiis remigandi laborem non intermiserunt: itaque

310 longarum navium cursum adaequârunt. 31. Accessum

est ad Britanniam omnibus navibus meridiano fere

tempore, neque in eo loco hostis est visus: sed, ut

Caesar postea ex captivis cognovit, quum magnae

manus eò convenissent, multitudine navium perterriti

315 erant; statim a litore discesserant ac se in superiora

loca abdiderant. Caesar exercitum exposuit et

locum castris idoneum cepit: ex captivis cognovit,

Caesar lands his troops. quo in loco hostium copiae conse-
The enemy are discov-
ered in a forest inland. dissent: cohortibus decem praesidio
Caesar dislodges them.
320   navibus Q. Atrium praefecit. Ad

mare reliquit et equites trecentos, qui praesidio

navibus essent. Ipse de tertiâ vigiliâ ad hostes

contendit. Noctu progressus millia passuum circiter

duodecim, hostium copias conspicatus est. 32. Illi,

325 equitatu atque essedis ad flumen progressi, ex loco

superiore nostros prohibere et proelium committere

coeperunt. Repulsi ab equitatu se in silvas abdide-

Slinger
(Schreiber-Anderson)

Sling-bolts
(Schreiber-Anderson)

Testudo (Schreiber-Anderson)

runt, locum nacti egregie et natura et opere munitum:
nam, crebris arboribus succisis, omnes introitus erant
praeclusi. Ipsi ex silvis rari propugnabant, nostrosque 330
intra munitiones ingredi prohibebant. At milites
legionis septimae, testudine factâ, et aggere ad munitiones adjecto, locum ceperunt: eosque ex silvis
expulerunt, paucis vulneribus acceptis. Sed eos fugi-
entes longius Caesar prosequi vetuit: nam loci naturam 335
ignorabat: magna pars diei jam consumpta erat;
munitioni castrorum tempus relinqui volebat.

33. Postero die mane, tripartito milites equitesque
Next day he is pre- in expeditionem misit, ut eos, qui fuge-
vented from pursuit
by the news that the rant persequerentur. Hi aliquantum 340
fleet had been nearly
destroyed by a gale in itineris progressi sunt, et jam paene
the night.
erant in prospectu hostium; sed
equites a Q. Atrio ad Caesarem venerunt, qui
nuntiarent superiore nocte, maxima coorta tempestate, prope omnes naves afflictas atque in litore 345
ejectas esse, quod neque ancorae funesque subsisterent,
neque nautae gubernatoresque vim tempestatis pati
possent: itaque ex eo concursu navium magnum
incommodum esse acceptum dixerunt.

34. His rebus cognitis, Caesar legiones equitatumque 350
Working night and day revocari atque in itinere resistere
for ten days, the
Romans repair their jubet, ipse ad naves revertitur: eadem
fleet, which is safely
beached. fere, quae ex nuntiis litterisque
cognoverat, coram perspicit: naves circiter quadraginta erant amissae: reliquae tamen refici posse 355

magno negotio videbantur. Itaque ex legionibus fabros deligit, et ex continenti alios arcessi jubet: ipse, etsi res erat multae operae ac laboris, tamen commodissimum esse statuit omnes
360 naves subduci, et cum castris unâ munitione conjungi: in his rebus circiter dies decem consumit: ne noctu quidem labor intermittitur: naves subducunt, et castra egregie muniunt. 35. Tum Caesar easdem copias,

Caesar once more makes for the interior, where he finds the Britons gathering under Cassivellaunus. quas ante, praesidio navibus reliquit,
365 et eòdem, unde redierat, profectus est. Eò quum venisset, majores copiae Britannorum jam undique in eum locum convenerant: summa imperii bellique administrandi communi consilio Cassivellauno permissa
370 erat: cujus fines a maritimis civitatibus flumen dividit, quod appellatur Tamesis, a mari circiter millia passuum octoginta. Huic superiore tempore cum reliquis civitatibus continentia bella intercesserant; sed nostro adventu permoti, Britanni hunc
375 toti bello imperioque praefecerant.

36. Insula naturâ est triquetra, cujus unum latus

Description of Britain. est contra Galliam. Hujus lateris alter angulus, quò fere omnes ex Galliâ naves appelluntur, ad orientem solem, inferior ad
380 meridiem spectat. Hoc pertinet circiter millia

Dimensions, &c. passuum quingenta. Alterum vergit ad Hispaniam atque occidentem solem: quâ ex parte est Hibernia, dimidio minor, ut aestimatur, quam

Britannia, sed pari spatio transmissus atque ex
Gallia est in Britanniam. In hoc medio cursu est 385
insula, quse appellatur Mona: complures praeterea
insulae minores subjectae esse existimantur: de
quibus insulis nonnulli scripserunt dies continuos
triginta sub brumâ esse noctem. 37. Nos nihil de eo
percontationibus reperiebamus, nisi certis ex aquâ 390
mensuris breviores esse quam in continenti noctes
videbamus. Hujus lateris est longitudo, ut fert
illorum opinio, septingentorum millium. Tertium
est contra septentriones: cui parti nulla est objecta
terra, sed ejus angulus lateris maxime ad Germaniam 395
spectat. Hoc millia passuum octingenta in longi-
tudinem esse existimatur. Ita omnis insula est in
circuitu vicies centum millium passuum.

Britanniae pars interior ab iis incolitur, quos natos
esse in insulâ ipsi dicunt: maritima Its inhabitants, and 400
pars ab iis, qui praedae ac belli products.
inferendi causâ ex Belgis transierunt: (qui omnes fere
iis nominibus civitatum appellantur, quibus orti ex
civitatibus eò pervenerunt): et, bello illato, ibi perman-
serunt, atque agros colere coeperunt. 38. Hominum 405
est infinita multitudo, creberrimaque aedificia, fere
Gallicis consimilia; pecorum magnus est numerus.
Utuntur aut aere aut taleis ferreis ad certum pondus
examinatis pro nummo. Nascitur ibi plumbum
album in mediterraneis regionibus: in maritimis 410
ferrum, sed ejus exigua est copia: aere utuntur

importato. Materia cujusque generis ut in Galliâ est praeter fagum atque abietem. Leporem et galli- nam et anserem gustare fas non putant: haec tamen
415 alunt animi voluptatisque causâ. Loca sunt tempera- tiora quam in Galliâ, remissioribus frigoribus.

39. Ex his gentibus longe sunt humanissimi, qui Cantium incolunt: quae regio est mari- tima omnis, neque multum a Gallicâ
420 differunt consuetudine. Interiores plerique frumenta non serunt, sed lacte et carne vivunt, pellibusque sunt vestiti. Omnes vero se Britanni vitro inficiunt, quod caeruleum efficit colorem, atque hoc horridiores sunt in pugnâ aspectu; capillum habent promissum;
425 omnem corporis partem praeter caput et labrum superius radunt.

Manners and customs of the Britons.

Equites hostium essedariique acriter proelio cum equitatu nostro in itinere conflix- erunt: nostri tamen omnibus parti-
430 bus superiores fuerunt, atque eos in silvas collesque compulerunt: sed, compluribus interfectis, cupidius insecuti nonnullos ex suis amiserunt. 40. At illi, intermisso spatio, subitò se ex silvis ejecerunt, impetumque in eos fecerunt, qui erant in statione
435 pro castris collocati. Nostri autem imprudentes erant atque in munitione castrorum occupati: hostes acriter pugnaverunt: et, nostris novo genere pugnae perterritis, per medios audacissime perruperunt, seque inde incolumes receperunt. Eo die Q. Laberius

An indecisive engage- ment with the Britons.

Durus, tribunus militum, interficitur. Illi, pluribus 440
cohortibus submissis, repelluntur.

Postero die procul a castris suis hostes in colli-
bus constiterunt: rari se ostenderunt: Followed next day by a great victory for the
et lenius quam pridie nostros equites Romans.
proelio lacessere coeperunt. 41. Sed meridie quum 445
Caesar pabulandi causâ tres legiones atque omnem equitatum cum Gaio Trebonio legato misisset, repente ex
omnibus partibus ad pabulatores advolaverunt, sic uti
ab signis legionibusque non absisterent. Nostri acriter
in eos impetu facto reppulerunt, neque finem sequendi 450
fecerunt, quoad subsidio confisi equites, quum post se
legiones viderent, praecipites hostes egerunt. Magnus
numerus hostium interfectus est: nam nostri iis
neque sui colligendi neque consistendi aut ex essedis
desiliendi facultatem dederunt. Ex hâc fugâ protinus 455
quae undique convenerant auxilia discesserunt; neque
post id tempus unquam summis copiis nobiscum
hostes contenderunt.

42. Caesar, cognito consilio eorum, ad flumen Tame-
sim in fines Cassivellauni exercitum Caesar crosses the 460
Thames.
duxit: quod flumen uno omnino loco
pedibus, atque hoc aegre, transiri potest. Eò quum
venisset, vidit magnas hostium copias ad alteram flumi-
nis ripam esse instructas. Ripa autem erat acutis sudi-
bus munita; sudesque ejusdem generis sub aquâ defixae 465
flumine tegebantur. Caesar, his rebus cognitis, equitatum praemittit: legiones confestim subsequi jubet.

Sed milites eâ celeritate atque eo impetu iêrunt, quum capite solo ex aquâ exstarent, ut hostes impetum 470 legionum atque equitum sustinere non possent: ripas dimiserunt ac se fugae mandaverunt.

43. Cassivellaunus omnem contentionis spem de-

Cassivellaunus, ponit: ampliores copias dimittit:
not wishing to risk
another battle, harasses millibus circiter quattuor essedario-
the Roman march by
475 irregular skirmishes rum relictis, itinera nostra servabat:
and ambuscades.
paulum ex viâ excedebat: locis impe-
ditis ac silvestribus se occultabat: in iis regionibus, quibus nos iter facturos esse cognoverat, pecora atque homines ex agris in silvas compellebat: tum, quum 480 equitatus noster praedandi vastandique causâ se in agros ejecerat, omnibus viis notis semitisque essedarios ex silvis emittebat: ita magno cum periculo nostrorum equitum cum iis confligebat, atque hoc metu latius vagari prohibebat. Itaque Caesar equites non longius 485 ab agmine legionum discedere passus est.

44. Interim Trinobantes, prope firmissima earum

The Trinobantes sub- regionum civitas, legatos ad Caesarem
mit to Caesar. Other
tribes follow. mittunt, pollicenturque sese ei dedi-
turos atque imperata facturos: ex quâ civitate 490 Mandubracius adolescens ad Caesarem in Galliam venerat: cujus pater in eâ civitate regnum obtinuerat, interfectusque erat a Cassivellauno: ipse fugâ mortem vitaverat. Illi petunt, ut Caesar Mandubracium ab injuriâ Cassivellauni defendat, atque in civitatem 495 mittat. His Caesar imperat obsides quadraginta,

frumentumque exercitui; Mandubraciumque ad eos mittit. Illi imperata celeriter fecerunt: obsides ad numerum frumentumque miserunt.

45. Ita Caesar Trinobantes defendit atque milites ab omni injuria prohibuit: mox etiam Cenimagni, Segontiaci, Ancalites, Bibroci, Cassi, legationibus missis, Caesar's attack on Verulamium (St. Albans), the stronghold Cassivellaunus. 500

sese Caesari dedunt. Ab his cognoscit non longe ex eo loco oppidum Cassivellauni abesse, silvis paludibusque munitum, quò magnus hominum pecorisque numerus convenerit. Oppidum autem Britanni vocant, quum silvas impeditas vallo atque fossâ muniêrunt, quò incursionis hostium vitandae causâ convenire consuêrunt. Eò proficiscitur cum legionibus: locum reperit egregie naturâ atque opere munitum: tamen hunc duabus ex partibus oppugnare contendit. Hostes, paulisper morati, militum nostrorum impetum non tulerunt, seseque aliâ ex parte oppidi ejecerunt. Magnus ibi numerus pecoris repertus est: multique in fugâ sunt comprehensi atque interfecti. 505 510 515

46. Dum haec in his locis geruntur, Cassivellaunus ad Cantium, quibus regionibus quattuor reges praeerant, Cingetorix, Carvilius, Taximagulus, Segovax, nuntios mittit: his imperat, ut, coactis omnibus copiis, castra navalia de improviso Cassivellaunus urges the four chieftains of Kent to attack the camp on the shore. Defeat of the Britons. Cassivellaunus himself submits to Caesar. 520

oppugnent. Ii quum ad castra venissent, nostri eruptionem fecerunt: multos eorum interfecerunt:

Lugotorigem, ducem nobilem, ceperunt. Cassivellau-
525 nus, hoc proelio nuntiato, tot detrimentis acceptis,
vastatis finibus, maxime etiam defectione civium per-
motus est: legatos per Atrebatem Commium de dedi-
tione ad Caesarem mittit. Caesar, quum constituisset
hiemare in continenti propter repentinos Galliae motus,
530 neque multum aestatis superesset, obsides imperat:
constituit quid vectigalis in singulos annos populo
Romano Britannia penderet: imperat Cassivellauno,
ne Mandubracio neu Trinobantibus noceat.

    47. Obsidibus acceptis, exercitum reducit ad mare,
535 Caesar returns to Gaul naves invenit refectas. His deductis,
to winter quarters.
           quòd et captivorum magnum nume-
rum habebat, et nonnullae tempestate deperierant
naves, duobus commeatibus exercitum reportare
instituit. Ac sic accidit, ut ex tanto navium numero,
540 tot navigationibus, neque hoc neque superiore anno,
ulla omnino navis, quae milites portaret, desideraretur:
at ex iis, quae inanes ex continenti ad eum remitte-
bantur, militibus prioris commeatus expositis, per-
paucae locum ceperunt: reliquae fere omnes rejectae
545 sunt. Quas quum aliquamdiu Caesar frustra expecta-
visset, ne anni tempore a navigatione excluderetur,
quòd aequinoctium suberat, necessario angustius
milites collocavit: summa tranquillitas consecuta est:
initâ vigiliâ secundâ, naves solvit: primâ luce terram
550 attigit omnesque incolumes naves perduxit.

NOTES

The Numbers refer to lines of the Text.

3. **Proficisci statuit**. Caesar was at this time in N. Gaul: he had just been fighting the Suevi and other tribes near the Rhine.

6. **loca**. The usual plural form of **locus: loci** means *topics, places in books* generally.

13. **ea**, acc., object of **reperire**.

16. **navi longa**, a ship of war. Roman ships of war were long and narrow to ensure speed.

18. **Morinos**. See map. The moat northerly people of Gaul. Virg. *Æn*. viii. 727, Extremique hominum Morini.

21. **Veneticum bellum**, the war with the Veneti. See map. They were a sea-faring tribe, and had possessed a large fleet, which Caesar had just destroyed in battle.

26. **dare...obtemperare**. Verbs like volo, possum, videor, etc., are incomplete in meaning without an infinitive, which is called *complementary*.

imperio. Dat. after obtempero = I am obedient *to*.

29. **Commium**. A Gaulish king, chief of the tribe of the Atrebates. They had been defeated by Caesar, and he had appointed Commius to be their king.

33. **magna**. Supply 'esse,' to be taken with **habebatur.**

37. **quae viderit**. **Viderit** is subjunctive because it is not stated as *fact*, but as a *representation* of Volusenus.

40. Legati. Legatus will be found in Caesar with *two* meanings, to be decided by the context: (1) a *herald* or *ambassador;* (2) a *lieutenant-general,* or *adjutant* to the Imperator.

42. populo. Dat. case of the indirect object.

45. propter anni tempus. The summer was growing late. It was now towards the end of August.

47. His. Dat. of indirect object.

48. eos in fidem recipit = 'receives their submission.'

49. cogit = 'presses into his service.'

50. numero. Abl. of respect.

52. quaestores. The **quaestores** had charge of all money matters: they sometimes took command.

legatis. See above, l. 40(2). Caesar had ten *legati* in Gaul. They were sometimes entrusted with separate commands.

praefectis. The **praefecti militum** commanded the auxiliary troops, or had special duties apart from the legion.

53. accedebant = came = 'were added.'

54. ab millibus passuum. **Mille passus** or **millia passuum** = 1000 paces, 1600 English yards. **Ab** here denotes not merely *distance* or *separation* from, but also the measure of the distance. Translate, 'at a distance of eight miles from,' etc.

61. tertia vigilia. The period between sunset and sunrise was divided into four equal parts called *vigilia,* distinguished as *prima, secunda, tertia, quarta vigilia,* each *vigilia* containing three *horae noctis.* Of course the length of the *vigiliae* varies, being longest in winter, and shortest in summer.

62. ulteriorem portum. If Caesar sailed from Itius, and if Itius is Wissant, this *ulterior portus* where the cavalry embarked should be Sangatte.

64. hora circiter quarta. The day would begin about 5 a.m., and this would therefore be about 9 o'clock. The Roman day from sunrise to sunset was divided into twelve equal parts, called *horae,* varying according to the season. **Circiter** is an adverb here.

69. **angustis** = 'precipitous.' **angustus** (from *ango*) = drawn in, contracted, hence 'having no slope.'

72. **nequaquam idoneus**, that is, for landing.

75. **tribunos militum** = military tribunes. There were six in each legion, but only one was on duty at a time. He had entire charge of the discipline when the soldiers were in camp.

77. **secundum. secundus** is really a participle from **sequor,** I follow: hence applied to wind and tide = favourable.

84. **essedarii. essedum**, from which **essedarii** comes, is a word of Gallic, not Latin, derivation: it was a two-wheeled chariot.

85. **hoc genere**. Abl. after **uti**. The verbs that take an abl. after them are **fungor, fruor, utor, vescor, dignor, potior**, and a few more: **uti** is complementary infinitive.

87. **reliquis copiis**. Abl. of *manner.* **subsecuti,** 'following closely.'

90. **in alto** = 'in deep water.' Caesar means that the ships drew so much water that they could not be beached.

95. **ex arido** = 'from the dry beach.'

97. **insuefactos** = 'trained to go into the water.'

99. **imperiti** = 'inexperienced in.' Takes a gen. case.

105. **inusitatior** = 'somewhat strange.' Literally, 'stranger' (than the appearance of trading ships).

106. **motus ad usum expeditior** = 'their facility for steering was readier.'

107. **magno usui nostris fuit**. 'Sum' admits a *dat.* case as the *completion* of the *predicate* and a second dative of the *recipient.* Translate, 'was a great advantage to our men.'

110. **paulum modo** = 'for a short time only.' **pedem referre**, to retreat.

111. **militibus cunctantibus**. Abl. absolute. See Exercise xiii.

112. **decimae legionis**. The 10th legion, the 'Fighting Tenth,' contained the pick of Caesar's troops. Under Caesar a legion consisted of about 3000 men. Each legion contained 10 cohorts of 300 men;

each cohort 3 maniples of 100 men; and each maniple 2 centuries of 50. The men in each cohort stood ten deep. Usually on the field of battle the legion was drawn up in three lines. The principal standard of the legion was the eagle, which was carried by one of the bravest soldiers in the first cohort, under the charge of the centurion of the first century.

121. **pugnatum est ab utrisque** = **utrique pugnaverunt**. This impersonal use of pugnare is common.

123. **ordines servare** = 'to keep their ranks.'

124. **signa**. Besides the eagle, each division of the legion had its own standard, usually carried in front of the division.

alius alia ex navi = 'some from one ship and some from another.'

125. **quibuscumque,** etc. = 'whenever they had come up with a standard.'

129. **ab latere aperto** = 'in the undefended flank.'

131. **scaphas longarum navium** = 'the men-of-wars' cutters.' **Scapha** is a Greek word, meaning 'scooped out.'

Speculatoria navigia = 'reconnoitring vessels.'

132. **laborantes** = 'in distress.'

137. **insulam capere** = 'to reach the island.'

139. **simul atque** = 'as soon as.' See 1. 384 for explanation of **atque**.

146. **oratoris modo** = 'after the fashion of a herald.'

149. **ignosceretur**. Verbs taking a dat. in the active are used impersonally in the passive. Translate, 'that pardon might be granted to them.'

151. **quod...intulissent. Intulissent** is subjunctive, because it states, not a *fact*, but what Caesar *said* they had done.

164. **propius occasum**. The preposition **prope** takes an acc. case after it: so do **propior** and **proximus**, adjectives derived from **prope** and **propius**, adverb. **sui**, objective gen., 'with great peril to themselves.'

166. **adversa nocte** = 'as the night was unfavourable to them.'

168. **luna plena**. This full moon has been fixed as having happened on the night of the 30th and 31st August, B.C. 55.

170. **incognitum**. Because there are no tides in the Mediterranean.

174. **administrandi** = 'managing the ships.'

186. **Romanis. Sum** with its compounds, except **possum**, takes a dat.

189. **hoc…quod** = 'for this reason … because.' **hoc** is abl.

191. **frumento prohibere**. Verbs of *preventing* take an abl.: observe also **reditu interclusis**.

198. **ex eventu navium** – 'from what had happened to his ships.' Objective gen.

199. **ex eo quod** = 'from the fact that.'

204. **ex continenti**. Understand **terra**: *continuous, unbroken* land as opposed to an island.

208. **Dum ea geruntur. Dum** (= while) always takes the present indicative.

209. **frumentatum**. The supine in **um** is used to express a *purpose* after verbs of motion.

214. **in ea parte…quam in partem** = 'in that direction towards which': this superfluous addition of the noun in a relative sentence is not uncommon in Caesar. Compare i. 16, **diem instare, quo die**, etc.

215. **aliquid novi consilii**. The genitive after **aliquid, multum, plus, nihil**, is commoner than those words in agreement with the succeeding noun.

228. **incertis ordinibus** = 'the ranks being broken.'

230. **ex essedis** has the force of an adjective agreeing with *pugnae*.

234. **turmas**. The cavalry attached to each legion numbered 300, divided into 10 squadrons (*turmae*) of 30 each.

243. **temonem…jugum**, 'the chariot-pole,' 'the yoke to hold the horses' necks together.'

248. **receperunt se** = 'recovered themselves.'

250. **post aliquid temporis**. See l. 215–216.

252. **reliqui** = the rest of the Britons.

254. **dies**. Acc. of *duration* of time.

258. **daretur**. Subjunctive in *indirect* question. See Exercise xxxiii.

267. **pro castris** = as a defense to the camp.

269. **spatio brevi** = at a short interval.

273. **His**. Dat. with notion of disadvantage.

274. **quem imperaverat** = which he had imposed: **imperare** with dat. of *person* and acc. of *thing* is common in this sense.

279. **infra** = to the south.

284. **ex litteris** = 'in accordance with Caesar's despatches.'

285. **supplicatio**. When a general at the head of his army won a victory, the senate decreed a public thanksgiving (*supplicatio*) to the gods for a number of days in proportion to the greatness of the victory.

286. **Trevirorum**. The Treviri, who have given their name to Trèves or Trier, occupied a part of the district of the Belgæ between the Moselle and the Rhine.

288. **ad portum Itium**. The chief place of the Morini in those days: most probably the place now called Wissant.

292. **Corus**. A wind from the W.N.W.

298. **pari…quem**. **Par** is more frequently followed by *ac* or *quam*. Here it seems to be used like **idem** which is followed by *qui*. Translate—'with an equal number of cavalry to that which he had left.'

300. **Africo**. A wind from the W.S.W.

301. **circiter** is an adverb here: **nocte**, abl. of time *when*.

307. **esset**. Subjunctive, because it states not an actual *fact,* but a *possibility.*

316. **exposuit** = disembarked.

318. **consedissent**. Subjunctive in *indirect* question.

319. **cohortibus.** Dat. after **praefecit**. **praesidio**, dat. of *purpose.* **navibus**, dat. of *recipient.*

322. **de tertia vigilia**. **de** seems to mean 'at the beginning of.'

325. **equitatu**. Abl. of manner. **ad flumen**. Possibly the Stour.

330. **rari** = 'in scattered knots.'

332. **testudine facta**. In attacking a wall or rampart the Roman soldiers locked their shields together over their heads for a protection against missiles from above. This was called a **testudo** or 'tortoise.'

332. **aggere adjecto**. **agger** was a bank of earth carried up to the base of the ramparts.

338. **mane**. An old indeclinable noun, used in the nom., acc., and abl. cases.

344. **nuntiarent**. Subj. expressing purpose, **qui** = **ut ei**.

346. **subsisterent** = 'maintained their hold.'

351. **resistere** = 'to halt.'

352. **eadem fere,** etc. = 'personally sees that the facts were almost as he had ascertained,' etc.

358. **multae operae**. *Gen.* of quality describing **res**.

360. **subduci** = 'to be beached.'

369. **Cassivellaunus** ruled over the country N. of the Thames. He was the most powerful chieftain of these parts, and to him was entrusted the supreme command of the British forces.

371. **Tamesis**. The Thames. Caesar reckons its distance from the coast by the length of his march from the coast to where he crossed, *i.e.*, 80 miles.

383. **dimidio**. Abl. of *measure*.

384. **transmissus**. Nom. case. **pari...atque,** 'the passage is of *about the same* length *as* it is from Gaul, etc.' **par...ac** is like **idem** or **simul ac**. The explanation of **ac** here is simple: *e.g.*, take **simul ac venit, vicit** = 'as soon as he came he conquered.' The full form was **simul vicit ac simul venit** = 'he came *and* conquered at the same time.' The phrase was afterwards shortened to **simul ac venit, vicit**.

386. **Mona**. Tacitus speaks of Anglesey under this name: but from the position Caesar must be referring to the Isle of Man. The **insulae minores** are probably islands on the W. coast of Scotland.

389. bruma. Contracted from **brevima,** old form of superlative *brevissima*: *i.e.,* time when the day is shortest—winter.

390. ex aqua mensuris. The clepsydron, a contrivance by means of which time is measured by water dropping from one vessel into another.

392. ut opinio fert, as their opinion is.

400. ipsi = 'the inhabitants themselves.'

402. Belgis. There was a tribe called Belgae in Britain occupying parts of Hampshire and Sussex.

403. iis ... pervenerunt = 'are called by the names of those tribes from which they originated before they came there:' for **civitatum, quibus ex civitatibus** see above, l. 214.

408. taleis ferreis = 'bars of iron.'

409. plumbum album = 'tin'; but Caesar cannot be correct in saying that it is found in the midland districts, as the tin mines of Cornwall are older than any historical record. Iron was worked in Sussex (*maritimis regionibus*), as it was until long after Caesar's time. Bronze probably came from Gaul.

415. animi causâ = 'for the sake of amusement.'

422. vitro = 'woad,' a plant used for dyeing blue.

427. The preceding remarks about Britain have been a diversion: the account is now resumed from the point where it was dropped in c. 35.

441. submissis = 'sent to their relief.'

443. rari = 'in scattered parties.'

447. C. Trebonio. Tribunus plebis B.C. 55, now a *legatus* under Caesar, was afterwards one of his assassins.

454. sui colligendi = 'of rallying themselves.'

457. summis copiis = 'with all their forces together.'

459. consilio. This was to fall back on the river Thames.

461. uno loco...transiri potest. See Introduction, p. xvii.

465. defixae = fastened down under the water.

475. servabat = 'kept our route in sight.'

479. quum...ejecerat. *Quum* may take the pluperf. indicative when a demonstrative (as **tum** here) precedes, more accurately marking the time.

482. **periculo nostrorum**, etc. Obj. gen. after **periculo**.

483. **hoc metu** = by fear of this.

485. **agmine**. *agmen* is the line of march: *acies*, the line of battle.

486. **Trinobantes**. The people of Essex.

487. **firmissima** = most warlike. *Civitas*. Caesar uses rather loosely for both Gallic and British tribes.

494. **Cassivellauni**. Subjective gen., after **injuria**.

495. **His…imperat**. See above, l. 274.

497. **ad numerum** = 'to the required number.'

501. The **Cenimagni** probably came from Norfolk, Suffolk, and Cambridge: the **Segontiaci** from parts of Hampshire and Berks: the **Ancalites** from Wilts: the **Bibroci** from Berks: the **Cassi** from Herts. The position of some of these tribes is very doubtful, but Berks seems to preserve the name of the **Bibroci**, and Cassiobury that of the **Cassi**.

504. **oppidum**: afterwards occupied by the Romans, who built the town of Verulamium upon it, the site of the present St. Albans.

531. **quid vectigalis**. See l. 216.

533. **neu**. **ne** repeated becomes **neu**, not **neque**.

541. **quae milites portaret** = for carrying soldiers. This is the force of the subjunctive here, which indicates a purpose.

543. **prioris commeatus** = of the former voyage.

547. **aequinoctium**. Caesar left Britain before the last week of September.

549. **vigilia secunda**. See l. 61.

abl., ablative.
acc., accusative.
adj., adjective.
adv., adverb.
comm., common.
comp., comparative.
conj., conjunction.
dat., dative.
defect., defective.
demons., demonstrative.
distrib., distributive.
f., feminine.
frequent., frequentative.
gen., genitive.
gov., governing.
imper., imperative.
impers., impersonal.
incept., inceptive.
indecl., indeclinable.
indef., indefinite.
infin., infinitive.
irreg., irregular.
lit., literally.

m., masculine.
n., neuter.
nom., nominative.
num., numeral.
part., participle.
pass., passive.
perf., perfect.
pl., plural.
poss., possessive.
prep., preposition.
pres., present.
pron., pronoun.
pronom., pronominal.
reflex., reflexive.
rel., relative.
sing., singular.
subst., substantive.
superl., superlative.
v. dep., verb deponent.
v.i., verb intransitive.
voc., vocative.
v.t., verb transitive.

VOCABULARY
(Latin–English)

ab *or* **a,** *prep. gov. abl.*, by, from, away.

ab·d-o, -ere, **·dĭd**-i, **·dĭt**-um, *v.t.* 3, I hide.

abi-es, -ĕtis, *f.*, a pine tree, fir.

ab·sist-o, -ere, **·stĭt**-i, **·stĭt**-um, *v.i.* 3, I stand apart from.

ab·sum, ·esse, ·fui, *v.i.*, I am away, I am distant.

ac (at-que), *conj.*, and.

ac·cēd-o, -ere, **·cess**-i, **·cess**-um, *v.i.* 3, I approach, I am added (ad; cedo, I go).

accept-us, *from* accipio.

access-um est, *from* accedo, it was approached.

ac·cĭd-o, -ere, -i (no supine), *v.i.* 3, to fall out, to happen (ad, upon; cado, I fall).

ac·cĭp-io, -ere, **·cēp**-i, **·cēpt**-um, *v.t.* 3, I receive (ad; capio, I take).

aci-es, -ei, *f.*, order *or* line of battle.

acrĭter, *adv.*, sharply, vigorously.

acūt-us, -a, -um, *adj.*, sharp, pointed.

ad, *prep. gov. acc.*, to, at, towards, for.

ad·aeq-uo, *v.t.* 1, I bring to an equality, I keep pace with (ad, to; aequo, I make equal).

ad·dūc-o, -ere, **·dux**-i, **·duct**-um, *v.t.* 3, I lead to, I bring to.

ad·eo, ·ire, ·iv-i, *or* **i**-i, **·ĭt**-um, *v.i. irreg.*, I go to, I approach.

ad·ig-o, -ere, **·ĕg**-i, **·act**-um, *v.t.* 3, I drive to, I hurl to (ad; ago, I drive).

adĭt-us, -ūs, *m.*, a means of approach.

ad·jic-io, -ere, **·jec**-i, **·ject**-um, *v.t.* 3, I throw upon, I add.

ad·ministr-o, *v.t.* 1, I manage, I carry out.

admodum, *adv.*, very, exceedingly.

adolesc-ens, -entis, *comm. gen.*, a youth.

ad·or-ior, -iri, -tus sum, *v. dep.* 4, I attack.

advent-us, -ūs, m., arrival (advenio, I come to).

advers-us, -a, -um, opposite, unfavourable.

ad·vol-o, *v.i.* 1, I fly to, I hasten.

aedific-ium, -ii, *n.*, a building.

aedific-o, *v.t.* 1, I build.

aegre, *adv.*, with difficulty, scarcely.

aequinoct-ium, -ii, *n.*, the equinox (aequus, equal; nox, night).

ae-s, -ris, *n.*, bronze, copper.

aest-as, -atis, *f.*, summer.

aestim-o, *v.t.* 1, I estimate, I reckon.

aes-tus, -tūs, *m.*, the tide.

af·flict-o, *v.t.* 1, I toss (ad, to; fligo, I dash).

afflict-us, *from* affligo.

af·flīg-o, -ere, **·flix**-i, **·flict**-um, *v.t.* 3, I shatter, I damage (ad, to; fligo, I dash).

Afric-us, -i, *m.*, the south-west wind.

ager, agr-i, *m.*, a field, territory.

agg-er, -ĕris, *m.*, a mound.

ag·grĕg-o, *v.t.* 1, I flock to, I attach myself to (ad; grex, a flock).

ag-men, -mĭnis, *n.*, a march, a column (of soldiers).

ag-o, -ere, **ēg**-i, **act**-um, *v.t.* 3, I do, I drive.

alacrĭt-as, -ātis, *f.*, alacrity, ardour.

alb-us, -a, -um, *adj.*, white.

ali-ēnus, -ēna, -ēnum, *adj.*, belonging to another, unfavorable.

aliquamdiu, *adv.*, for a considerable time.

aliquant-um, -i, *n.*, somewhat, some portion. **aliquant**-us, -a, -um, *adj.*, some.

alĭ·quis, alĭ·quid (*fem. sing.* and *neut. pl.* not used), somebody, something.

al-ĭus, -ĭa, -ĭud, *adj.*, another (*gen.*, alīus; *dat.*, alii).

alii…alii, some…others.

al-o, -ere, -ui, -ĭtum *and* –tum, *v.t.* 3, I rear, I keep.

al-ter, -tera, -terum (*gen.*, al-**tĕrĭus;** *dat.*, al-tĕri), *adj.*, the one (of two); **alter…alter,** the one…the other

alt-ĭtūdo, -ĭtūdĭnis, *f.*, depth.

alt-um, -i, *n.*, the deep, the open sea, (alt-us, high, deep).

amiss-us, *from* amitto.

a·mitt-o, *v.t.* 3, I lose (*see* mitto).

ampl-ior, -ius, *comp. adj.*, the greater (amplus).

Ancălĭt-es, -um, *m. pl.*, the Ancalites.

ancŏr-a, -ae, *f.*, an anchor.

angŭl-us, -i, *m.*, an angle, a corner.

angust-ior, *comp. of* angustus.

angustius, *compar. adv.*, more closely.

angust-us, -a, -um, *adj.*, narrow, contracted, steep.

anim·advert-o, -ere, -i, **·advers**-um, *v.t.* 3, I observe, I understand (animum, the mind; **adverto,** I turn towards).

anim-us, -i, *m.*, mind, amusement.

ann-us, -i, *m.*, a year.

ans-er, -ĕris, *m.*, a goose.

ante, *adv.*, before, previously; *prep. gov. acc.*, before.

antea, *adv.*, previously, once.

apert-us, -a, -um, *adj.*, uncovered, exposed, (aperio, to uncover).

appell-o, *v.t.* 1, I call.

ap·pell-o, -ere, **·pul**-i, **·puls**-um, *v.t.* 3, I drive to, I bring to.

ap·propinqu-o, *v.i.* 1, I draw near to, I approach (with *dat.*).

aqu-a, -ae, *f.*, water.

aquil-a, -ae, *f.*, an eagle.

aquĭlĭf-er, -eri, *m.*, a standard bearer (aquila, an eagle; fero, I carry).

arbitr-or, *v. dep.* 1, I think, I consider.

arb-or, -ŏris, *f.*, a tree.

ar·cess-o, -ere, -īvi, -ītum, *v.t.* 3, I call, I send for (ad, to; cedo, I go, I cause to go).

arĭd-um, -i, *n.*, dry land (aridus, dry).

arm-a, -orum, *n. pl.*, arms, weapons.

armament-a, -orum, *n. pl.*, tackling.

arm-o, *v.t.* 1, I arm, I furnish with arms.

aspect-us, -ūs, *m.*, appearance.

at, *conj.*, but, yet.

at·ting-o, -ere, **·tĭg**-i, **·tact**-um, *v.t.* 3, I touch on, I reach (ad; tango, I touch).

atque, *conj.*, as, with (*after words denoting similarity*), (*see* ac).

Atrĕb-as, -ătis, *m.*, one of the Atrebates.

auctor-ĭtas, -itatis, *f.*, influence, authority.

audacissime, *superl. adv.*, very boldly (audacter).

audacter, *adv.*, boldly (audax, bold).

aud-eo, -ere, **aus**-us sum, *v. semi-dep.* 2, I dare.

aurīg-a, -ae, *m.*, a driver, a charioteer.

aut, *conj.*, or. **aut...aut,** either...or.

autem, *conj.*, but, moreover.

auxīli-or, *v. dep.* 1, I help.

auxil-ium, -ii, *n.*, help, succour.

barbăr-us, -i, *m.*, a barbarian.

Belg-ae, -ārum, *m. pl.*, the Belgae, the Belgians.

bell-um, -i, *n.*, a war, warfare.

Bibroc-i, -orum, *m. pl.*, the Bibroci.

brev-ior, -ius, *comp. adj.*, shorter (brevis).

brev-is, -e, *adj.*, short, small (*comp.*, **brev**-ior; *superl.*, **brev**-issimus).

Britann-ia, -iae, f., Britain.

Britann-i, -orum, *m. pl.*, the Britons.

brum-a, -ae, *f.*, winter.

C = **Cai**-us, -i, *m.*, Gaius.

caerule-us, -a, -um, *adj.*, deep blue.

Caes-ar, -ăris, *m.*, Caesar.

Caius, -i, *m.*, Gaius.

Cant-ium, -ii, *n.*, Cantium, Kent.

cap-illus, -illi, *m.*, the hair (caput, the head).

cap-io, -ere, **cēp**-i, **capt**-um, *v.t.* 3, I take, I reach, I seize, I capture.

cap-tīvus, -tīvi, *m.*, a prisoner (capio, I take).

cap-ut, -ĭtis, *n.*, the head.

car-o, -nis, *f.*, flesh.

Carvil-ius, -ii, *m.*, Carvilius.

Cass-i, -orum, *m. pl.*, The Cassi.

Cassivellaun-us, -i, *m.*, Cassivellaunus.

cas-us, -ūs, *m.*, chance, accidents (cado, I fall).

castr-a, -ōrum, *n. pl.*, a camp.

caus-a, -ae, *f.*, a cause, a reason.

caus-â, *adverbial abl.* (with *gen.* or *gerund* in –di), for the purpose of.

celer-ĭtas, -ĭtātis, *f.*, swiftness, speed (celer, swift).

celĕrĭter, *adv.*, quickly.

Cenimagn-i, -orum, *m. pl.*, the Cenimagni.

centum, *num. adj. indecl.*, a hundred.

cep-it, *from* capio.

certe, *adv.*, surely.

cert-us, -a, -um, *adj.*, certain, sure.

Cingĕtŏr-ix, -ĭgis, *m.*, Cingetorix.

circiter, *adv.*, about, nearly.

circuit-us, -ūs, *m.*, a circumference.

circum·d-o, -are, **·dĕd**-i, **·dăt**-um, *v.t.* 1, I surround.

circum·sist-o, -ere, **·stĕt**-i, (no supine), *v.t.* 3, I stand round, I surround.

citissĭme, *superl. adv.*, with the utmost rapidity (cito, rapidly).

civ-is, -is, *comm. gen.*, a citizen.

civ-ītas, -itātis, *f.*, a state.

clam, *adv.*, secretly, by stealth.

class-is, -is, *f.*, a fleet.

co·act-a, *from* cogo.

coep-io, -isse, -i, -tum, *def.*, *v.t.* and *n.* 3, I begin.

cognĭt-us, *from* cognosco.

co·gnosc-o, -ere, **·gnŏv**-i, **·gnĭt**-um, *v.t.* 3, I make inquiry about, I ascertain. In perf. tense, I know.

cognov-erat, *from* cognosco.

cō·g-o, -ere, **co·ēg**-i, **co·act**-um, *v.t.* 3, I collect, I compel (cum, together; ago, I drive).

cohor-s, -tis, *f.*, a cohort.

col·lĭg-o, -ere, **·lēg**-i, **·lect**-um, *v.t.* 3, I gather together, I collect (con; lego, I gather).

coll-is, -is, *m.*, a hill.

col·loc-o, *v.t.* 1, I put, I place (con; loco, I place).

col·loqu-or, -i, **·loquut**-us sum, *v. dep.* 3, I talk with, I confer with (con; loquor, I speak).

col-o, -ere, -ui, **cult**-um, *v.t.* 3, I cultivate, I till.

cŏl-or, -ōris, *m.*, colour.

commeā-tus, -tūs, *m.*, supplies, provisions, a voyage.

com·mend-o, *v.t.* 1, I commit, I entrust.

com·mitt-o, *v.t.* 3, I entrust (with *dat.*), I engage in.

Comm-ius, -ii, *m.*, Commius.

commode, *adv.*, advantageously.

commodissim-us, -a, -um, *superl. adj.*, most convenient, very advantageous.

com·mor-or, *v. dep.* 1, I delay, I stop.

commun-is, -e, *adj.*, common.

commuta-tio, -tiōnis, *f.*, a change, an alteration.

com·păr-o, *v.t.* 1, I prepare.

com·pell-o, -ere, **·pŭl**-i, **·puls**-um, *v.t.* 3, I drive together, I force.

com·plĕ-o, **·plēre**, **·plēv**-i, **·plēt**-um, *v.t.* 2, I fill up.

com·plur-es, -a, *adj.*, very many, several.

com·port-o, *v.t.* 1, I carry together, I collect.

com·prehend-o, -ere, -i, **·pre-hens**-um, *v.t.* 3, I seize.

comprehens-us, *from* comprehendo.

concil-ium, -ii, *n.*, a meeting, a council.

concurs-us, -ūs, *m.*, a running together, a collision (concurro).

con·fer-o, -re, **·tul**-i, **collat**-um, *v.t. irreg.*, I bring together, I collect, I attribute to.

confert-us, -a, -um, *adj.*, crowded together, close packed.

confestim, *adv.*, immediately.

con·fīd-o, -ere, **·fīs**-us sum, *v.t. semi-dep.* 3, I am persuaded, I am confident, *v.i.*, I rely upon.

con·firm-o, *v.t.* 1, I strengthen, I establish.

confis-us, *perf. part. of* confido.

con·flīg-o, -ere, **·flix**-i, **·flict**-um, *v.i.* 3, I come into conflict, I engage (con; fligo, I dash).

con·jĭc-io, -ere, **·jēc**-i, **·ject**-um, *v.t.* 3, I throw, I hurl.

con·jung-o, -ere, **·junx**-i, **·junct**-um, *v.t.* 3, I join together, I unite.

con·jura-tio, -tiōnis, *f.*, a plot (con; juro, I swear).

con·scend-o, -ere, -i, **·scens**-um, *v.t.* 3, I embark, I go on board (con; scando, I mount).

con·sĕqu-or, *v. dep.* 3, I follow after, I pursue (*see* sequor).

con·sĭd-o, -ere, **·sēd**-i, **·sess**-um, *v.i.* 3, I take my station, I encamp.

consil-ium, -ii, *n.*, a plan, a purpose, intention, counsel.

con·simil-is, -e, *adj.*, quite like (with *dat.*).

con·sist-o, -ere, **·stit**-i, **stĭt**-um, *v.i.* 3, I halt, I stop, I take my stand.

con·spĭc-io, -ere, **·spex**-i, **·spect**-um, *v.t.* 3, I see, I observe.

con·spĭc-or, *v. dep.* 1, I see, I descry.

constit-erunt, *from* consisto.

con·stitu-o, -ere, -i, **·stitūt**-um, *v.t.* 3, I put, I station, I appoint, I draw up, I determine.

consu-erunt, *from* consuesco.

consuē-sco, -scere, -vi, -tum, *v.i. incep.* 3, I accustom myself.

consue-tūdo, -tudĭnis, *f.*, custom, habit.

consuev-it, *from* consuesco.

con·sum-o, -ere, **·sumps**-i, **·sumpt**-um, *v.t.* 3, I spend, I pass.

con·tend-o, -ere, -i, **·tent**-um, *v.i.* and *a.* 3, I strive, I contend, I proceed eagerly, I hasten.

content-io, -iōnis, *f.*, a contest.

con·test-or, *v. dep.* 1, I call to witness, I invoke.

continen-s, -tis, *f.*, the connected land, the mainland (continēre, to be continuous).

continen-s, -tis, *pres. part. of* contineo, continuous, constant.

con·tin-eo, *v.t.* 2, I confide, I shut in, I restrain (con, teneo).

con·tin-uus, -ua, -uum, *adj.*, in succession (con; teneo, I hold).

contra, *prep. gov. acc.*, against, opposite to.

con·vĕn-io, -ire, ·**vēn**-i, ·**vent**-um, *v.i.* 4, I come together, I assemble.

con·vŏc-o, *v.t.* 1, I call together, I assemble.

co·or-ior, -iri, -tus sum, *v. dep.* 4, I arise.

coort-us, *from* coorior.

cop-ia, -iae, *f.*, a supply, plenty, a quantity; *plural*, forces, troops.

coram, *adv.*, personally; *prep.*, in the presence of.

corp-us, -ŏris, *n.*, a body.

Cor-us, -i, *m.*, Corus, *i.e.*, the north-west wind.

creb-er, -ra, -rum, *adj.*, frequent, numerous, many.

creberrim-us, -a, -um, *superl. adj.*, very frequent, very numerous (creber, frequent).

culp-a, -ae, *f.*, a fault.

cum, *prep. gov. abl.*, with.

cunct-or, *v. dep.* 1, I delay, I hesitate.

cupidius, *compar. adv.*, more eagerly, too eagerly (cupide).

curr-us, -ūs, *m.*, a chariot, (curro, I run).

cur-sus, -sūs, *m.*, a running, a course (curro, I run).

dare, *see* do.

daretur, *from* do.

dat-urus, *from* do.

de, *prep. gov. abl.*, from, out of, concerning, during.

de improviso, unexpectedly.

decem, *num. adj. indecl.*, ten.

de·cern-o, -ere, ·**crēv**-i, ·**crēt**-um, *v.t.* 3, I decree, I decide.

dĕc-ĭmus, -ĭma, -ĭmum, *num. adj.*, tenth.

declīv-is, -e, *adj.*, sloping.

dēdĕc-us, -ŏris, *n.*, a disgrace, a dishonor.

ded-ērunt, *from* do.

dēdit-io, -iōnis, *f.*, a surrender (dedo).

de·d-o, -ere, ·**dĭd**-i, ·**dĭt**-um, *v.t.* 3, I give up, I surrender.

de·duc-o, (*see* subduco), *v.t.* 3, I lead off, I withdraw, I launch.

deduct-us, *from* deduco.

defect-io, -iōnis, *f.*, a revolt, a defection.

de·fend-o, -ere, -i, **·fens**-um, *v.t.* 3, I protect.

de·fer-o, *v.t. irreg.*, I bring down, I carry down (*see* fero).

de·fīg-o, -ere, **·fix**-i, **·fix**-um, *v.t.* 3, I fix down, I drive down.

de·inde, *adv.*, afterwards, then.

de·jic-io, -ere, **·jēc**-i, **·ject**-um, *v.t.* 3, I throw down, I drive down (de, down).

de·lat-us, *from* defero.

dē·līg-o, *v.t.* 1, I bind down, I fasten.

de·lig-o, -ere, **·lēg**-i, **·lect**-um, *v.t.* 3, I choose out, I select.

de·litesc-o, -ere, **·lit**-ui (no supine), *v.i.* 3, I conceal myself (de, away; latesco, I hide myself).

de·met-o, -ere, **·mess**-ui, **·mess**-um, *v.t.* 3, I mow, I cut down.

de·monstr-o, *v.t.* 1, I show, I point out.

de·per-eo, -ire, **·iv**-i *or* **·i**-i (no supine), *v.i.*, I am entirely destroyed.

dē·pon-o, -ere, **·pos**-ui, **·posīt**-um, *v.t.* 3, I lay down, I lay aside, I give up.

desidĕr-o, *v.t.* 1, I desire, I miss (a thing).

de·sil-io, -ire, -ui, **·sult**-um, *v.i.* 4, I leap down.

dē·sum, ·esse, ·fu-i, *v.i. irreg.*, I fail, I am wanting.

detriment-um, -i, *n.*, loss, damage.

de-us, -i, *m.*, a god.

dic-o, -ere, **dix**-i, **dict**-um, *v.t.* 3, I say.

di-es, -ei, *m.* and *f.*, a day, a time.

dif·fer-o, -re, **dis·tul**-i, **dī·lat**-um, *v.i. irreg.*, I am different.

difficul-tas, -tātis, *f.*, difficulty.

dimidi-um, -i, *n.*, a half.

dī·mitt-o (*see* mitto), *v.t.* 3, I send about, I dismiss, I quit.

dis·cēd-o, -ere, **·cess**-i, **·cess**-um, *v.i.* 3, I depart.

discess-erant, *from* discedo.

dis·perg-o, -ere, **·pers**-i, **·pers**-um, *v.t.* 3, I disperse (dis, in different directions; spargo, I scatter).

dis·trĭbu-o, -ere, -i, **·tribūt**-um, *v.t.* 3, I distribute, I assign (dis, among several; tribuo, I give).

diūtĭus, *adv.*, longer (*compar. of* diu).

dīvĭd-o, -ere, **divīs**-i, **divīs**-um, *v.t.* 3, I divide.

dix-erunt, *from* dico.

d-o, -are, **dĕd**-i, **dăt**-um, *v.t.* 1, I give, I put.

dom-us, -i, and, -ūs, *f.*, a house, a home.

duc-o, -ere, **dux**-i, **duct**-um, *v.t.* 3, I lead.

dum, *conj.* whilst, until.

du-o, -ae, -o, *num. adj. pl.*, two.

duŏ·decim, *num. adj. indecl.*, twelve.

duodeviginti, *adj.*, eighteen.

duplĭc-o, *v.t.* 1, I double.

Dur-us, -i, *m.*, Durus.

dux, duc-is, *comm. gen.*, a leader, a chief.

e *or* **ex**, *prep. gov. abl.*, from, out of, away from, according to.

effect-urus, *from* efficio.

ef·fic-io, -ere, **·fēc**-i, **·fect**-um, *v.t.* I make, I carry out, I bring to pass.

ef·fŭg-io, -ere, **·fūg**-i, **·fugĭt**-um, *v.t. and n.* 3, I flee away, I escape.

ego, *pers. pron.*, I.

e·grĕd-ior, -i, **·gress**-us sum, *v. dep.* 3, I disembark.

egrĕgie, *adv.*, excellently, exceedingly well, strongly.

e·gress-us, *from* egredior.

egress-us, -ūs, *m.*, a landing-place.

ejicere se (*see* ejicio), to throw themselves out, to rush forth.

e·jic-io (*see* adjicio), *v.t.* 3, I cast out, I drive ashore.

e·mitt-o, (*see* mitto), *v.t.* 3, I send out.

enim, *conj.*, for.

eo, *adv.*, thither, there, for this reason.

eo, ire, iv-i, *or* **i**-i, **ĭt**-um, *v.i. irreg.*, I go.

eōdem, *adv.*, to the same place.

ĕqu-es, -ĭtis, *m.*, a horseman; *pl.*, cavalry.

ĕquit-ātus, *m.*, cavalry.

equ-us, -i, *m.*, a horse.

erupt-io, -iōnis, *f.*, a sortie, a sally (erumpo, I break out).

esse. *See* sum.

essed-ārius, -ārii, *m.*, a chariot warrior, charioteer.

essĕd-um, -i, *n.*, a war chariot.

et, *conj.*, and; **et...et,** both...and.

ĕtĭam, *conj.*, also even.

etsi, *conj.*, even if, although.

e·vĕn-io, -ire, **·vēn**-i, **·vent**-um, *v.i.* 4, I happen.

event-us, -ūs, *m.*, occurrence (evenire, to happen).

examin-o, *v.t.* 1, I weigh.

ex·ced-o, -ere, **·cess**-i, **·cess**-um, *v.i.*, 3, I go out, I withdraw.

ex·clud-o, -ere, **·clus**-i, **·clus**-um, *v.t.* 3, I prevent, I hinder (ex; claudo, I shut).

ex·cus-o, *v.t.* 1, I excuse.

exercitat-io, -iōnis, *f.*, exercise, practice.

exerc-ĭtus, -ĭtūs, *m.*, an army (exerceo, I exercise).

exigu-ĭtas, -ĭtātis, *f.*, small size (exiguus, small).

exigu-us, -a, -um, *adj.*, small, little.

ex·istim-o, *v.t.* 1, I think, I suppose (ex; aestimo).

expedī-tio, -tiōnis, *f.*, an expedition.

ex·pedīt-us, -a, -um, *part.*, unimpeded, ready, easy (*comp.*, expeditior).

ex·pell-o, -ere, **·pul**-i, **·puls**-um, *v.t.* 3, I drive out, I expel.

ex·pon-o, -ere, **·posu**-i, **·posĭt**-um, *v.t.* 3, I post, I draw up (ex, out, forth; pono, I place).

exposit-us, *from* expono, here = landed.

expos-uit, *from* expono.

ex·pul-erunt, *from* expello.

exspect-o, *v.t.* 1, I wait, I await.

ex·st-o, -are, (*no perf. or supine*), *v.i.* 1, I stand out of.

fa-ber, -bri, *m.*, an artificer.

faci-endae, *from* facio.

făc-io, -ere, **fēc**-i, **fact**-um, *v.t.* 3, I make.

fact-us, *from* facio.

facul-tas, -tātis, *f.*, power, opportunity.

fag-us, -i, *f.*, a beech tree, beech.

fas, *n. indecl.*, the will of the gods, a lawful thing.

felīcĭter, *adv.*, prosperously.

fĕre, *adv.*, nearly, almost, about.

fer-o, -re, **tul**-i, **lāt**-um, *v.t. irreg.*, I bear, I carry.

ferre. *See* fero.

ferr-eus, -ea, -eum, *adj.*, made of iron, iron-.

ferr-um, -i, *n.*, iron.

fert, *from* fero.

fid-ēlis, -ēle, *adj.*, faithful.

fĭd-es, -ei, *f.*, faith, engagement, protection.

figūr-a, -ae, *f.*, a form, a shape, appearance.

fin-is, -is, *m.*, an end, a boundary; *pl.*, borders, territory.

firm-issimus, -issima, -issimum, *superl. adj.*, strongest, most powerful (firmus).

firmĭter, *adv.*, firmly.

flect-o, -ere, **flex**-i, **flex**-um, *v.t.* 3, I turn.

fl-o, *v.i.* 1, I blow.

fluct-us, -ūs, *m.*, a wave.

flu-men, -mĭnis, *n.*, a river (fluo, I flow).

fore, *from* sum.

fortun-a, -ae, *f.*, chance, fortune.

foss-a, -ae, *f.*, a ditch, a trench.

frang-o, -ere, **frēg**-i, **fract**-um, *v.t.* 3, I break, I wreck.

frig-us, -ŏris, *n.*, cold, coldness.

frument-or, *v. dep.* 1, I get corn, I forage.

frument-um, -i, *n.*, corn.

frustra, *adv.*, in vain.

fug-a, -ae, *f.*, flight.

fŭg-io, -ere, **fūg**-i, **fŭgĭt**-um, *v.i. and a.* 3, I flee.

fund-a, -ae, *f.*, a sling.

fun-is, -is, *m.*, a rope, a cable.

Gall-i, -orum, *m. pl.*, the Gauls.

Gall-ia, -iae, *f.*, Gaul.

Gallĭc-us, -a, -um, *adj.*, Gallic.

gallīn-a, -ae, *f.*, a hen.

gen-s, -tis, *f.*, a race, a nation, a people.

gen-us, -ĕris, *n.*, a race, a kind.

German-ia, -iae, *f.*, Germany.

gĕr-o, -ere, **gess**-i, **gest**-um, *v.t.* 3, I carry on, I do, I wage.

grav-is, -e, *adj.*, heavy.

gravissime, *adv.*, very seriously (*superl. of* graviter).

gubernā-tor, -tōris, *m.*, a pilot.

gust-o, *v.t.* 1, I taste.

hab-eo, *v.t.* 2, I have, I hold, I consider.

hibern-a, -ōrum, *n. pl.*, winter quarters.

Hibern-ia, -iae, *f.*, Ireland.

hic, haec, hoc, *demons. pron.*, this.

hiem-o, *v.i.* 1, I winter, I take up winter quarters (hiems, winter).

hiem-s, -is, *f.*, winter.

Hispan-ia, -iae, *f.*, Spain.

hoc, *adverbial abl.*, on this account.

hom-o, -ĭnis, *comm. gen.*, a man, a person.

hōr-a, -ae, *f.*, an hour.

horrid-ior, -ius, *compar. adj.*, more terrible, more horrible (horridus).

hort-or, *v. dep.* 1, I exhort, I encourage.

hos-tis, -tis, *comm. gen.*, an enemy.

huc, *adv.*, hither.

human-issimus, -issima, -issimum, *superl. adj.*, most civilized (humanus).

ibi, *adv.*, there.

ī·dem, eă·dem, ĭ·dem, *demons. pron.*, the same.

ĭdōne-us, -a, -um, *adj.*, suitable, convenient.

ignōr-o, *v.t.* 1, I am unacquainted with.

i·gnosc-o, -ere, **·gnov**-i, **·gnot**-um, *v.t. and n.* 3, I pardon, I overlook (*with dat.*), (in, not; nosco, I know).

i·gnōt-us, -a, -um, *adj.*, not known, unknown (nosco).

illat-um, *from* infero.

ill-e, -a, -ud, *pron. demons.*, he, she, it, that.

illò, *adv.*, to that place, thither.

impĕdi-mentum, -menti, *n.* (*pl.*), baggage.

im·ped-io, *v.t.* 4, I impede, I hinder (in; pes, a foot).

impedīt-us, *past part.*, impedio, obstructed.

imperā-tor, -tōris, *m.*, a commander, a general.

imperat-um, -i, *n.*, a command.

im·perīt-us, -a, -um, *adj.*, unskilful, not acquainted with (*with gen.*).

impĕr-ium, -ii, *n.*, dominion, empire, a command.

imper-o, *v.t.* 1, I command, I order.

impĕt-us, -ūs, *m.*, an attack, an onset.

im·port-o, *v.t.* 1, I carry into, I import.

im·prōvīs-us, -a, -um, *adj.*, unexpected (in, not; provideo, I foresee). **de improviso**, unexpectedly.

im·prud-ens, -entis, *adj.*, heedless, unwary (in, not; prudens, foreseeing).

im·prudent-ia, -iae, *f.*, imprudence, indiscretion.

in, *prep. with acc.*, into, for, against; *with abl.*, in, on, at, upon.

inān-is, -e, *adj.*, empty.

in·cend-o, -ere, -i, **·cens**-um, *v.t.* 3, I set on fire, I burn.

in·cert-us, -a, -um, *adj.*, uncertain.

incitat-us, -a, -um, *adj.*, *past part.*, at full speed, swift (incito).

in·cĭt-o, *v.t.* 1, I set in rapid motion, I urge forward.

in·cognĭt-us, -a, -um, *adj.* unknown, (in, not; cognitus, known).

incŏl-a, -ae, *comm. gen.*, an inhabitant.

in·col-o, -ere, -ui, (*no supine*), *v.i. and a.* 3, I dwell, I inhabit.

in·colūm-is, -e, *adj.*, quite safe, in safety.

incommod-um, -i, *n.*, trouble, disaster.

incur-sio, -siōnis, *f.*, an inroad, a raid (in; curro, I run).

inde, *adv.*, from that place, thence.

in·eo, ·ire, ·iv-i *or* **·ĭt**-um, *v.t. irreg.*, I form, I adopt, I begin.

infer-ior, -ius, *comp. adj.*, lower.

in·fer-o, -re, **·tul**-i, **il·lat**-um, *v.t.*, I bring into, I make (war).

in·fic-io, -ere, **·fēc**-i, **·fect**-um, *v.t.* 3, I dip in, I dye.

infinīt-us, -a, -um, *adj.*, countless, infinite.

infra, *adv.*, below.

in·grĕd-ior, -i, **·gress**-us, sum; *v. dep.* 3, I enter.

inĭt-us, *from* ineo.

injuri-a, -ae, *f.*, injustice, a wrong.

inquam, *v. def.*, I say.

in·sequ-or, *v. dep.* 3, I follow after.

in·sinu-o, *v.t.* 1, I make a way into (in; sinuo, I wind).

in·sist-o, -ere, **·stĭt**-i (*no supine*), *v.i.* 3, I stand.

in·stitŭ-o, -ere, -i, **·stitūt**-um, *v.t.* 3, I resolve, I begin.

in·stru-o, -ere, **·strux**-i, **·struct**-um, *v.t.* 3, I build, I draw up (troops).

in·suĕ·fact-us, -a, -um, *adj.*, accustomed, *see* note (suesco, I accustom; facio, I make).

insŭl-a, -ae, *f.*, an island.

intellĭg-o, -ere, **·lex**-i, **·lect**-um, *v.t.* 3, I perceive, I understand.

inter, *prep. gov. acc.*, between, among.

inter·cēd-o, -ere, **·cess**-i, **·cess**-um, *v.i.* 3, I intervene, I am between.

inter·clud-o, -ere, **·clus**-i, **·clus**-um, *v.t.* 3, I close up, I cut off (inter, between; claudo, I shut).

interĕa, *adv.*, meanwhile.

interfect-us, *from* interficio.

inter·fic-io, -ere, **·fēc**-i, **·fect**-um, *v.t.* 3, I kill.

intĕrim, *adv.*, in the meantime.

inter-ior, -ius, *comp. adj.*, inner, interior.

intermiss-us, *from* intermitto, being allowed to intervene.

inter·mitt-o, (*see* mitto), *v.t.* 3, I leave off, I relax.

inter·pon-o, -ere, **·posui, ·pos**-ĭtum, *v.t.* 3, I interpose. *Pass.*, I arise (inter; pono, I place).

intra, *prep. gov. acc.*, within.

introĭt-us, -ūs, *m.*, an entrance, an approach.

in·usitāt-us, -a, -um, *adj.*, unusual, extraordinary (*comp.*, inusitatior).

in·util-is, -e, *adj.*, useless.

in·věn-io, (*see* venio), *v.t.* 4, I find, I discover.

ips-e, -a, -um, *pron.*, self, very; *as subst.*, himself.

is, ea, id, *pron.*, he, she, it, that.

ita, *adv.*, thus, so.

ita·que, *conj.*, and so, therefore.

item, *adv.*, so, also, in like manner.

i-ter, -tǐněris, *n.*, a march, a journey.

It-ius, -ii, *m.*, Itius.

jac-io, -ere, **jēc**-i, **jact**-um, *v.t.* 3, I throw.

jam, *adv.*, already, now.

jub-eo, -ere, **juss**-i, **juss**-um, *v.t.* 2, I order, I command.

jug-um, -i, *n.*, the yoke.

Laber-ius, -ii, *m.*, Laberius.

Labiēn-us, -i, *m.*, Labienus.

lab-or, -ōris, *m.*, toil, labor.

labor-o, *v.i.* 1, I labor, I am hard pressed.

labr-um, -i, *n.*, a lip.

lac, lact-is, *n.*, milk.

lacess-o, -ere, **·īv**-i, *or* **·i**-i, **·īt**-um, *v.t.* 3, I provoke, I attack.

late, *adv.*, widely.

lat-ius, *comp. adv.*, more widely.

lat-us, -ěris, *n.*, a side, a flank.

laud-o, *v.t.* 1, I praise.

legat-io, -ionis, *f.*, an embassy.

legāt-us, -i, *m.*, an ambassador, a lieutenant.

leg-io, -iōnis, *f.*, a legion.

lēn-is, -e, *adj.*, gentle.

lenius, *comp. adv.*, more slowly, with less spirit (leniter, slowly).

lěp-us, -ŏris, *m.*, a hare.

liberaliter, *adv.*, courteously, liberally.

liber-tas, -tātis, *f.*, liberty, freedom.

litter-a, -ae, *f. sing.*, a letter (of the alphabet); *pl.*, a letter, an epistle.

līt-us, -ŏris, *n.*, the sea-shore.

lŏc-us, -i, *m.* (*pl.* loc-i *and* loc-a), a place, a position.

longe, *adv.*, far off. **late,** *adv.*, widely. **longe lateque,** far and wide.

longinqu-us, -a, -um, *adj.*, far off, distant (*compar.*, longinquior).

longitūd-o, -ĭnis, *f.*, length.

longius, *adv.*, longer, farther.

long-us, -a, -um, *adj.*, long.

Lugotŏr-ix, -ĭgis, *m.*, Lugotorix.

lun-a, -ae, *f.*, the moon.

lux, luc-is, *f.*, light, daylight.

magn-itudo, -itudĭnis, *f.*, great-ness, magnitude.

magn·ŏpěre, *adv.*, greatly, exceedingly.

magn-us, -a, -um, *adj.*, great, large.

maj-or, -us, *comp. adj.*, greater.

mandāt-um, -i, *n.*, a command, an order.

mand-o, *v.t.* 1, I command, I commit.

Mandubra-cius, -ii, *m.*, Mandubracius.

mane, *adv.*, early in the morning.

man-us, -ūs, *f.*, a hand, a band (of men).

mar-e, -is, *n.*, the sea.

mar-itĭmus, -itĭma, - itĭmum, *adj.*, of the sea, sea-; on the sea-coast.

matĕr-ia, -iae, *f.*, wood, timber.

maxime, *superl. adv.*, in the highest degree, chiefly, very greatly.

maxĭm-us, -a, -um, *superl. adj.*, greatest, very great (magnus, great).

medi·terr-aneus, -anea, -aneum, *adj.*, inland.

med-ius, -ia, -ium, *adj.*, middle. **media nox,** midnight.

mensur-a, -ae, *f.*, a measuring, measurement.

mercāt-or, -ōris, *m.*, a trader.

merīdi-ānus, -āna, -ānum, *adj.*, of mid-day. **meridianum tempus,** mid-day.

meri·di-es, -ei, *m.*, mid-day, the south.

mĕt-o, (*see above*, de·meto), *v.t.* 3, I mow, I reap.

metŭ-o, -ere, -i (no sup.), *v.t. and n.* 3, I fear.

met-us, -a, -um, *poss. pron.*, my, mine.

mīl-es, -ĭtis, *comm. gen.*, a soldier.

milit-ia, -iae, *f.*, warfare.

milli-a, -um, *n. pl.*, a thousand.

min-or, -us, *compar. adj.*, less (*comp. of* parvus).

mis-erunt, *from* mitto.

miss-us, *from* mitto.

mitt-o, *v.t.* 3, I send.

mobīl-itas, -itatis, *f.*, quickness, rapidity (mobilis, easily moved).

modĕr-or, *v. dep.* 1, I manage, I control, I check.

modo, *adv.*, only, merely.

mod-us, -i, *m.*, a manner, a way.

Mon-a, -ae, *f.*, Mona.

mon-s, -tis, *m.*, a mountain.

morat-us, *from* moror.

Morĭn-i, -orum, *m. pl.*, the Morini.

mor-or, *v.t. dep.* 1, I delay, I linger, I tarry.

mor-s, -tis, *f.*, death.

mot-us, -ūs, *m.*, a motion, a movement.

mox, *adv.*, soon, afterwards.

mult-ĭtūdo, -ĭtūdĭnis, *f.*, a multitude, the mass of the people.

multum, *adv.,* much, greatly.
mul-tus, -ta, -tum, *adj.,* much.
mun-io, *v.t.* 4, I fortify, I pro-
    tect.
muni-tio, -tiōnis, *f.,* a fortifying,
    a fortification (munio).

nact-us, *from* nanciscor.
nam, *conj.,* for.
namque, *conj.,* for indeed.
nancisc-or, -i, **nact**-us sum, *v.*
    dep. 3, I get, I obtain.
nasc-or, -i, **nat**-us sum, *v. dep.* 3,
    I am born, I am produced.
natur-a, -ae, *f.,* the nature.
nav-ālis, -āle, *adj.,* naval, sea-.
naviga-tio, -tiōnis, *f.,* a sailing.
nav·ig-o, *v.i.* 1, I sail, (navis, a
    ship).
navǐg-ium, *n.,* a vessel.
nav-is, -is, *f.,* a ship.
naut-a, -ae, *m.,* a sailor.
ne, *adv.,* lest, that not.
ne quidem, not even.
necessārio, *adv.,* necessarily.
neglǐg-o, -ere, **neglex**-i,
    neglect-um, *v.t.* 3, I overlook,
    I neglect.
neg·ot-ium, -ii, *n.,* an affair,
    trouble (nec; otium, leisure).
nem-o, **nullius,** *n.,* nobody.
ne·quāquam, *adv.,* by no
    means.

nĕque, *conj.,* and not, nor;
    neque…neque,
    neither…nor.
neu, *conj.,* and not, nor.
nihil, *n. indecl.,* nothing.
nǐsǐ, *conj.,* if not, unless, except.
no·bilis, -bile, *adj.,* noble.
nobiscum = cum nobis.
noc-eo, *v.i.* 2, I hurt.
noct-es, *from* nox.
noctu, *adv. abl.,* by night.
nom-en, -ǐnis, *n.,* a name.
non, *adv.,* not.
nondum, *adv.,* not yet.
non·null-us, -a, -um, *adj.,*
    some.
non-us, -a, -um, *adj.,* ninth.
nos, *pl.* of ego.
nosc-o, -ere, **nōv**-i, **not**-um, *v.t.*
    3, I know.
nos-ter, -tra, -trum, *adj. pron.,*
    our; *as subst. pl. m.,* our men.
not-us, *perf. part. from* nosco.
nov·ǐtas, -ǐtātis, *f.,* newness,
    strangeness (novus, new).
nov-us, -a, -um, *adj.,* new.
nox, noct-is, *f.,* night.
n·ullus, ·ulla, ·ullum,
    adj., not any, none, no (ne,
    not; ullus).
numĕr-us, -i, *m.,* a number.
numm-us, -i, *m.,* money.
nunti-o, *v.t.* 1, I announce.

nunt-ius, -ii, *m.*, a messenger.

ob, *prep. gov. acc.*, for on account of.

ob.jic-io, -ere, **.jēc**-i, **.ject**-um, *v.t.* 3, I present (to view), I oppose (ob, before; jacio, I throw).

obs-es, -ĭdis, *comm.*, a hostage.

ob.tempĕr-o, *v.i.* 1, I submit to, I obey (*with dat.*).

ob.tin-eo, -ere, -ui, **.tent**-um, *v.t.* 2, I hold, I acquire.

occās-us, -ūs, *m.*, the setting *or* going down (ob; cado, I fall).

oc.cīd-o, -ere, -i, **.cīs**-um, *v.t.* 3, I cut down, I kill (ob, against; caedo, I strike).

oc.cĭd-o, -ere, -i, **.cās**-um, *v.i.* 3, I go down, I set.

occult-o, *v.t.* 1, I hide.

{ **oc.cup**-o, *v.t.* 1, I seize, I gain.

oc.cupat-us, *perf. part.*, engaged in.

oc.curr-o, -ere, -i, **.curs**-um, *v.i.* 3, I run up to, I fall in with, I meet (ob, towards; curro, I run).

ocĕăn-us, -i, *m.*, the ocean.

octingent-i, -ae, -a, *adj.*, eight hundred.

octo, *num. adj. indecl.*, eight.

octoginta, *num. adj.*, eighty.

offic-ium, -ii, *n.*, a duty, an office.

olim, *adv.*, at some time, formerly.

omn-ia, all things.

omnīno, *adv.*, altogether, wholly, in all.

omn-is, -e, *adj.*, all, every.

oner-arius, -aria, -arium, *adj.*, of *or* belonging to a burden (*see* note).

ŏn-us, -ĕris, *n.*, a burden, a load, a weight.

oper-a, -ae, *f.*, work, labour, aid.

opin-io, -iōnis, *f.*, opinion.

oppid-um, -i, *n.*, a town, a city.

opportun-issimus, -issima, -issimum, *superl. adj.*, most convenient, most opportune.

op.port-ūnus, -ūna, -ūnum, *adj.*, convenient, suitable, opportune.

op.prĭm-o, -ere, **.press**-i, **.press**-um, *v.t.* 3, I overwhelm, I overload (ob, against; premo, I press).

oppugn-o, *v.t.* 1, I attack, I besiege.

optim-us, -a, -um, *superl. adj.*, best.

op-us, -ĕris, *n.*, work, a fortification.

or-a, -ae, *f.*, the coast.

orā-tor, -tōris, *m.*, an ambassador.

ord-o, -ĭnis, *m.*, order, a line, a rank.

ori-ens, *pres. part. from* orior.

or-ior, -iri, -tus sum, *v. dep.* 3 *and* 4, I rise, I spring from.

ort-i, *from* orior.

ostend-o, -ere, -i, **osten**-sum, *and* –tum, *v.t.* 3, I show.

pabulat-or, -ŏris, *m.*, a forager.

pabul-or, *v. dep.* 1, I forage.

paene, *adv.*, nearly, almost.

pal-us, -ūdis, *f.*, a swamp, a marsh.

par, par-is, *adj.*, equal.

par-eo, *v.i.* 2, I obey (*with dat.*).

par-i, *from* par.

par-o, *v.t.* 1, I prepare, I procure.

par-s, -tis, *f.*, a part, a side.

pass-us, -ūs, *m.*, a step, a pace.

pass-us sum, *from* patior.

pat-ior, -i, **pass**-us sum, *v. dep.* 3, I bear, I endure, I suffer.

pauc-ĭtas, -ĭtātis, *f.*, a small number.

pauc-us, -a, -um, *adj.*, small; *pl.*, few.

paulatim, *adv.*, by little and little, gradually.

paulisper, *adv.*, for a short time.

paulo, *adv.*, a little, somewhat.

paulum, *adv.*, a little, somewhat.

pax, pac-is, *f.*, peace.

pecor-a, *from* pecus.

pec-us, -ŏris, *n.*, cattle.

ped-es, -itis, *m.* 3, a foot soldier; *pl.*, infantry.

peditāt-us, -ūs, *m.*, foot soldiers, infantry.

pell-is, -is, *f.*, a skin.

pell-o, -ere, **pepŭl**-i, **puls**-um, *v.t.* 3, I rout, I put to fight.

pend-o, -ere, **pepend**-i, *and* **pend**-i, **pens**-um, *v.t.* 3, I pay.

per, *prep. gov. acc.*, through, by, along.

percontat-io, -iōnis, *f.*, an enquiry.

per·curr-o, -ere, **·cucurr**-i, *or* **·curr**-i, **·curs**-um, *v.i.* 3, I run along.

per·duc-o, -ere, **·dux**-i, **·duct**-um, *v.t.* 3, I bring, I conduct.

per·ĕquĭt-o, *v.i.* 1, I ride through *or* hither and thither.

per·fĕr-o, -re, **·tul**-i, **·lat**-um, *v.t. irreg.*, I bear, I carry.

perīcŭl-um, -i, *n.*, an attempt, danger.

per·man-eo, -ere, -si, -sum, *v.i.* 2, I remain.

per·mitt-o, (*see* mitto), *v.t.* 3, I give up, I entrust, I allow.

per·mŏveo, *v.t.* 2, I move deeply, I stir (*see* summoveo).

per·pauc-us, -a, -um, *adj.*, very
little; *pl.*, very few.

per·rump-o, -ere, **·rūp**-i,
·rupt-um, *v.i.* 3, I break
through.

per·sequ-or, -i, **·secut**-us sum,
v. dep. 3, I pursue.

per·spic-io, -ere, **·spex**-i,
·spect-um, *v.t.* 3, I perceive, I
ascertain.

per·terr-eo, *v.t.* 2, I frighten
thoroughly, I terrify greatly.

per·tin-eo, -ere, -ui, **·tent**-um,
v.i. 2, I reach, I extend.

perturba-tio, -tiōnis, *f.*, confusion.

per·turb-o, *v.t.* 1, I disturb
utterly, I throw into confusion.

per·vĕn-io, (see venio), *v.i.* 4, I
come up, I arrive.

pes, pĕd-is, *m.*, a foot.

pĕt-o, -ere, -īvi, *and* –īi, ītum,
v.t. 3, I seek, I beg.

plan-us, -a, -um, *adj.*, level,
flat.

plē-nus, -na, -num, *adj.*, full
(pleo, I fill).

plerumque, *adv.*, for the most
part, generally.

**plerusque, pleraque,
plerumque**, *adj.*, the greater
part; *pl.*, very many.

plumb-um, -i, *n.*, lead.

plumbum album = tin.

plures. *See* plus.

plus, plur-is, *comp. adj.*, more;
pl., several, very many.

pol·lic-eor, -eri, -ītus sum,
v. dep. a. and n. 2, I promise.

pond-us, -ĕris, *n.*, a weight.

popul-us, -i, *m.*, the people.

port-a, -ae, *f.*, a gate.

port-o, *v.t.* 1, I carry.

port-us, -ūs, *m.*, a harbour.

pos·sum, po·sse, pot-ui, *v.
irreg.*, I am able, I can (potis,
able, *and* sum).

post, *prep. gov. acc.*, after,
behind.

post·ea, *adv.*, after that, afterwards.

post-erus, -era, -erum, *adj.*,
next, following.

prae·ceps, **·cip**-itis, *adj.*,
headlong, in headlong
flight (prae, before; caput,
the head).

prae·cep-s, **·cip**-ītis, *adj.*,
steep, precipitous (prae,
caput, head, foremost).

prae·clud-o, -ere, **·clus**-i,
·clus-um, *v.t.* 3, I close in front,
I block (prae; claudo, I shut).

pread-a, -ae, *f.*, booty, plunder.

prae·dic-o, *v.t.* 1, I declare, I
announce.

praed-or, *v. dep.* 1, I plunder.

praefect-us, -i, *m.*, a prefect, a commander.

prae·fic-io, -ere, **·fēc**-i, **·fect**-um, *v.t.* 3, I place over, I appoint to the command of (prae, before; facio, I make).

prae·miss-us, *from* praemitto.

prae·mitt-o, -ere, **·mīs**-i, **·miss**-um, *v.t.* 3, I send forward *or* in advance.

praesid-ium, -ii, *n.*, a protecting force, a garrison.

prae·st-o, -are, **·stĭt**-i, **·stĭt**-um, *v.t.* 1, I show, I perform, *v.i.*, I am superior.

prae·sum, ·esse, ·fui, *v.i.*, I am over, I rule.

praeter, *prep. gov. acc.*, except, besides.

praeterea, *adv.*, besides, moreover.

prĕm-o, -ere, **press**-i, **press**-um, *v.t.* 3, I press hard, I harass.

pridĭe, *adv.*, on the day before.

primo, *adv.*, at first, in the first place.

prīm-us, -a, -um, *adj.*, the first.

princ-eps, -ĭpis, *m.*, a chieftain, a leading man.

pri-or, -us, *comp. adj.*, former, previous.

pris-tĭnus, -tĭna, -tĭnum, *adj.*, former.

pro, *prep. gov. abl.*, before, instead of, as, for.

prob-o, *v.t.* 1, I approve, I think highly of.

pro·cēd-o, (succedo), *v.i.* 3, I go forwards, I advance.

prŏcul, *adv.*, at a distance, far off.

pro·d-o, -ere, **·dĭd**-i, **·dĭt**-um, *v.t.* 3, I give up, I surrender, I betray.

pro·duc-o, (*see* subduco), *v.t.* 3, I prolong.

proel-ium, -ii, *n.*, a battle.

proeli-or, *v. dep.* 1, I join battle, I fight.

pro·fect-us, *from* proficiscor.

pro·ficisc-or, -i, **·fect**-us sum, *v. dep.* 3, I set out.

pro·grĕd-ior, -i, **·gress**-us sum, *v. dep.* 3, I go forward, I advance, I proceed.

pro·gress-us, *from* progredior.

pro·hib-eo, *v.t.* 2, I hinder, I prevent, I protect.

pro·jic-io, -ere, **·jēc**-i, **·ject**-um, *v.t.* 3, I throw, I throw forward.

promiss-us, -a, -um, *adj.*, long, hanging down.

pro·mitt-o, *v.t.* 3, I send forward, I promise (*see* mitto).

prope, *prep.*, near; *adv.*, nearly.

pro·pell-o, -ere, **·pŭl**-i, **·puls**-um, *v.t.* 3, I propel, I drive forward, I push forward.

propius, *comp. adv.*, nearer, too near (prope, near).

propter, *prep. gov. acc.*, on account of, because of.

pro·pugn-o, *v.i.* 1, I go forth to fight, I make sallies.

pro·sequ-or, *v. dep.* 3, I follow after, I pursue (see sequor).

prospect-us, -ūs, *m.*, sight.

protĭnus, *adv.*, forthwith, immediately.

pro·vect-us, *from* proveho.

pro·veh-o, -ere, **·vex**-i, **·vect**-um, *v.t.* 3, I carry forwards, I carry along.

pro·vid-eo, (*see* video), *v.t.* 2, I foresee, I provide, I furnish.

proxĭm-us, -a, -um, *superl. adj.*, nearest, next.

Publ-ius, -ii, *m.*, Publius.

pugn-a, -ae, *f.*, a fight, a battle.

pugn-o, *v.t.* 1, I fight.

pulv-is, -ĕris, *m.*, dust.

put-o, *v.t.* 1, I think, I consider.

Q. = **Quint**-us, -i, *m.*, Quintus.

qua, *adv.*, in which place, where, wherever.

quadraginta, *num., adj., indecl.*, forty.

quaest-or, -ōris, *m.*, a quaestor.

quam, *adv.*, than.

quant-us, -a, -um, *adj.*, how great, how much.

quart-us, -a, -um, *adj.*, the fourth.

quattuor, *num. adj. indecl.*, four.

-que, *conj.*, and.

quĕr-or, -i, **quest**-us sum, *v. dep.* 3, I complain.

qui, quae, quod, *rel. pron.*, who, which, that.

qui·cumque, quae·cumque, quod·cumque, *rel. pron.*, whoever, whatever.

qui·dam, quae·dam, quod·dam, *indef. pron.*, some, certain.

quingent-i, -ae, *num. adj.*, five hundred.

quinque, *num. adj. indecl.*, five.

quin-tus, -ta, -tum, *num. adj.*, fifth.

Quintus, -i, *m.*, Quintus.

quis, quae, quid, *pron. interrog.*, who? what?

quis·quam, quae·quam, quic·quam *or* **quid·quam,** *pron. indef.*, any (person or thing).

quis·que, quae·que, quod·que, *adj. pron. indef.*, each, every.

quò, *adv.,* whither, where, in order that.

quo·ad, *adv.,* till, until.

quod, *conj.,* that, because that, inasmuch as.

quotidi-ānus, -āna, -ānum, *adj.,* daily.

quotidie, *adv.,* daily.

quuum, *adv.,* when; *conj.,* since, as, although.

rad-o, -ere, **ras**-i, **ras**-um, *v.t.* 3, I shave.

rar-us, -a, -um, *adj.,* dispersed here and there.

rebell-io, -iōnis, *f.,* a revolt.

recept-us, -ūs, *m.,* a retreat (recipio).

recipere se, to betake one's self, to recover one's self.

re·cip-io, -ere, ·**cēp**-i, ·**cept**-um, *v.t.* 3, I take back, I receive.

red·eo, ·**ire,** ·**īv**-i, *or* ·**ī**-i, ·**ĭt**-um, *v.i. irreg.,* I go back, I return.

rĕdĭt-us, -ūs, *m.,* a returning, a return (redeo, I return).

re·duc-o, -ere, ·**dux**-i, ·**duct**-um, *v.t.* 3, I lead back.

refect-us, *from* reficio.

re·fĕr·o, -re, **re·ttŭl**-i, **re·lat**-um, *v.t. irreg.,* I bring back, I carry back, I relate.

reficiend-as, *from* reficio.

re·fic·io, -ere, ·**fēc**-i, ·**fect**-um, *v.t.* 3, I repair.

reg-io, -iōnis, *f.,* a territory, a region.

regn-um, -i, *n.,* supreme power, a kingdom.

re·jic·io, -ere, ·**jēc**-i, ·**ject**-um, *v.t.* 3, I throw back.

relict-us, *from* relinquo.

re·linqu-o, -ere, ·**līqu**-i, ·**lict**-um, *v.t.* 3, I leave.

rĕlĭqu-us, -a, -um, *adj.,* left, remaining.

re·man-eo, -ere, -si (no supine), *v.i.* 2, I remain behind.

rem·ĭg-o, *v.i.* 1, I row (remus, an oar).

re·migr-o, (no perf. or supine), *v.i.* 1, I depart back, I return.

remiss-us, *part. perf. pass.* (remitto), mild, not severe.

re·mitt-o, -ere, ·**mīs**-i, ·**miss**-um, *v.t.* 3, I send back.

re·mŏv-eo, -ere, -i, ·**mōt**-um, *v.t.* 2, I remove, I withdraw.

rēm-us, -i, *m.,* an oar.

re·nunti-o, *v.t.* 1, I bring back work, I report.

re·pell-o, -ere, ·**ppŭl**-i, ·**puls**-um, *v.t.* 3, I drive back, I repulse.

repente, *adv.,* suddenly.

repentīn-us, -a, -um, *adj.,* sudden, unexpected.

re·pĕr-io, -ire, **rep·per**-i,
  re·pert-um, *v.t.* 4, I find out,
  I discover.
repert-us, *from* reperio.
report-o, *v.t.* 1, I carry back.
re-s, -i, *f.*, a thing, an affair, a
  circumstance.
re·sist-o, -ere, **·stit**-i (*no supine*),
  v.i. 3, I withstand, I halt.
res·publica, rei·publicae, *f.*,
  the commonwealth.
re·vert-or, -i, **·vers**-us sum, *v.*
  dep. 3, I return.
re·voc-o, *v.t.* 1, I call back, I
  recall.
rex, rēg-is, *m.*, a king.
rip-a, -ae, *f.*, a bank.
Rom-a, -ae, *f.*, Rome.
Romān-us, -a, -um, *adj.*, Roman.
rot-a, -ae, *f.*, a wheel.
Ruf-us, -i, *m.*, Rufus.
rursus, *adv.*, back again, again.

sagitt-a, -ae, *f.*, an arrow.
satis, *adv.*, sufficiently, enough.
scaph-a, -ae, *f.*, a boat.
scrīb-o, -ere, **scrips**-i, **script**-um,
  v.t. 1, I write.
se (*or* **sese**), *reflex. pron.*, *sing.*
  and pl., himself, herself,
  itself, themselves.
secum, with himself (*cum is*
  written after and joined to

pers. pron.).
secund-us, -a, -um, *adj.*, favor-
  able, second.
secut-us, *from* sequor.
sed, *conj.*, but.
Segon-ax, -ācis, *m.*, Segonax.
Segontĭăc-i, -orum, *m. pl.*, the
  Segontiaci.
sēmĭt-a, -ae, *f.*, a path.
senāt-us, -ūs, *m.*, the Senate.
septem, *num. adj. indecl.*,
  seven.
septentri-o, -ōnis (*most fre-*
  quently pl.), *m.*, the north.
sept-īmus, -īma, -īmum, *num.*
  adj., seventh.
septingent-i, -ae, -a, *num. adj.*,
  seven hundred.
sĕqu-or, -i, **sequut**-us sum *or*
  secut-us sum, *v. dep.* 3, I
  follow.
sĕr-o, -ere, **sēv**-i, **săt**-um, *v.t.* 3,
  I sow.
serv-o, *v.t.* 1, I keep, I watch.
sese. *See* se.
si, *conj.*, if.
sic, *adv.*, so, thus. **sicuti,** to
  such a degree that (*see* ut).
sign-um, -i, *n.*, a signal, a (military) standard.
silv-a, -ae, *f.*, a wood.
silv-estris, -estre, *adj.*, woody
  (silva).

sĭmul, *adv.,* together, at once, at the same time.

simul atque, as soon as.

sine, *prep. gov. abl.,* without.

singulăr-is, -e, *adj.,* single, solitary.

singul-i, -ae, -a, *num. distrib. adj.,* separate, single, each.

sinistr-a, -ae, *f.,* the left hand.

sol, sol-is, *m.,* the sun.

sol-eo, -ere, -ĭtus sum, *semi-dep.* 2, I am wont, I am accustomed.

solĭt-us, -a, -um, *adj.,* usual, ordinary (soleo, I am accustomed).

sol-us, -a, -um, *adj.,* alone, only.

solv-o, -ere, -i, **solut**-um, *v.t.* 3, I loosen (se, apart; luo, I loosen).

spat-ium, -ii, *n.,* space, distance, interval of time.

speci-es, -ēi, *f.,* an appearance.

spect-o, *v.t.* 1, I look at, or towards.

speculator-ius, -ia, -ium, *adj.,* pertaining to a spy or scout.

spe-s, -i, *f.,* hope, expectation.

stabil-ĭtas, -itatis, *f.,* steadiness (stabilis, steady).

statim, *adv.,* immediately.

stat-io, -iōnis, *f.,* a station, an outpost.

stătŭ-o, -ere, -i, **statūt**-um, *v.t.* 3, I decide, I determine.

strepĭt-us, -ūs, *m.,* a noise.

stud-ium, -ii, *n.,* eagerness, energy.

sub, *prep. gov. abl. and acc.,* under, below, near, during.

sub·dūc-o, -ere, **·dux**-i, **·duct**-um, *v.t.* 3, I draw ashore (sub, from below; duco, I draw).

subĭto, *adv.,* suddenly.

sub·jic-io, -ere, **·jec**-i, **·ject**-um, *v.t.* 3, I throw under, I place near.

sub·ministr-o, *v.t.* 1, I supply, I furnish.

sub·mitt-o, *v.t.* 1, I send, I dispatch (*see* mitto).

sub·sĕqu-or, *v. dep.* 3, I follow close after, I follow in close pursuit.

subsid-ium, -ii, *n.,* aid, assistance, a support.

sub·sist-o, -ere, **·stĭt**-i, **·stĭt**-um, *v.i.* 3, I hold out.

sub·sum, ·esse, ·fui, *v.i.,* I am near, I am at hand.

suc·cēd-o, -ere, **·cess**-i, **·cess**-um, *v.i.* 3, I go in the place of, I succeed (sub; cedo, I go).

suc·cīd-o, -ere, -i, **·cis**-um, *v.t.* 3, I cut down (sub; caedo, I cut).

sud-es, -is, *f.,* a stake.

Sulpic-ius, -ii, *m.,* Sulpicius.

sum, esse, fu-i, *v.i. irreg.,* I am.

summ-a, -ae, *f.*, the whole, the chief.

sum·mŏv-eo, -ere, **·mōv**-i, **·mōt**-um, *v.t.* 2, I drive away (sub, from beneath; moveo, I move).

summ-us, -a, -um, *superl. adj.*, highest, greatest, very great (*superl.* of superus).

superat-us, *from* supero.

super-ior, -ius, *adj.*, higher, upper, former, superior (*comp.* of superus).

super-o, *v.t.* 1, I overcome, I subdue, I conquer.

super·sum, **·esse**, **·fui**, *v.i.*, I remain, I am left.

supplicat-io, -iōnis, *f.*, a thanksgiving.

suspic-io, -iōnis, *f.*, mistrust, suspicion.

suspĭc-or, *v. dep.* 1, I mistrust, I suspect.

sus·tin-eo, -ere, -ui, **·tent**-um, *v.t.* 2, I support, I check.

sustul-erant, *from* tollo.

su-us, -a, -um, *poss. pron.*, his own, her own, its own.

tale-a, -ae, *f.*, a rod, a bar.

tamen, *adv.*, nevertheless, yet.

Tamĕs-is, -is, *m.*, the Thames.

tandem, *adv.*, at length, at last.

tant-us, -a, um, *adj.*, so much, so great.

Taximăgul-us, -i, *m.*, Taximagulus.

tĕg-o, -ere, **tex**-i, **tect**-um, *v.t.* 3, I cover.

tel-um, -i, *n.*, a weapon, a javelin.

tem-o, -ōnis, *m.*, the pole (of a carriage).

temperat-ior, -ius, *comp. adj.*, more temperate, milder.

tempes-tas, -tātis, *f.*, a time, a season, a storm.

temp-us, -ŏris, *n.*, time, season.

ten-eo, *v.t.* 2, I hold, I detain, I keep.

terg-um, -i, *n.*, the back.

terr-or, -ōris, *m.*, alarm, terror.

ter-tius, -tia, -tium, *adj.*, the third.

test-ūdo, -ūdĭnis, *f.*, a covering, a shed.

tim-or, -ōris, *m.*, fear, terror.

toll-o, -ere, **sus·tul**-i, **sub·lat**-um, *v.t.* 3, I lift up, I carry away.

torment-um, -i, *n.*, a military engine.

tot, *num. adj. indecl.*, so many.

tot-us, -a, -um, *adj.*, the whole (*gen.*, totīus; *dat.*, toti).

traject-us, -ūs, *m.*, a crossing, passage.

tranquillit-as, -ātis, *f.*, calmness, a calm.

trans·eo, -ire, **·iv**-i *or* **·i**-i, **·it**-um, *v.t. irreg.*, I go across, I cross over.

trans·miss-us, -ūs, *m.*, a passage (across the sea), (trans, across; mitto, I send).

transport-o, *v.t.* 1, I carry over, I transport.

Trebon-ius, -ii, *m.*, Trebonius.

tre·cent-i, -ae, -a, *num. adj.*, three hundred.

tres, tria (*gen.*, trium), *num adj.*, three.

Trēvĭr-i, -orum, *m.*, the Treviri.

trib-ūnus, -ūni, *m.*, a tribune.

triginta, *num. adj. indecl.*, thirty.

Trinobant-es, -um, *m. pl.*, the Trinobantes.

tripartīto, *adv.*, in three divisions.

triquetr-us, -a, -um, *adj.*, triangular.

tu-eor, -eri, -ītus sum, *v. dep.*, 2, I protect, I defend.

tul-erunt, *from* fero.

tul-it, *from* fero.

tum, *adv.*, then.

turm-a, -ae, *f.*, a troop, a squadron.

ubi, *adv.*, when, where.

ull-us, -a, -um, *adj.*, any.

ulter-ior, -ius, *comp. adj.*, further.

una, *adv.*, at one and the same time, together.

unde, *adv.*, whence.

undĭque, *adv.*, from all parts.

unĭvers-us, -a, -um, *adj.*, all together, the whole.

unquam, *adv.*, at any time, ever.

un-us, -a, -um, *adj.*, one.

u-sus, -sūs, *m.*, use, experience (utor).

ut (*or* **uti**), *adv. as conj.*, that, so that, in order that.

uter·que, utră·que, utrum·que, *pron. adj.*, both, each; as *subst. pl.*, both sides.

ut-or, -i, **us**-us sum, *v. dep.* 3, I use, I employ (*with abl.*).

vad-um, -i, *n.*, a shallow.

vag-or, *v. dep.* 1, I wander.

vall-um, -i, *n.*, a rampart.

vast-o, *v.t.* 1, I lay waste, I devastate, I plunder.

vectīg-al, -ālis, *n.*, a tax, tribute.

vector-ius, -ia, -ium, *adj.*, for carrying.

Vĕnĕt-ĭcus, -ĭca, -ĭcum, *adj.*, of *or* belonging to the Veneti.

vĕn-io, -ire, **vēn**-i, **vent**-um, *v.t.* 4, I come.

ventĭt-o, *v.i. frequent.* 1, I keep coming.

vent-us, -i, *m.*, wind.

verg-o, -ere (*no perf. or supine*),
   v.i. 3, I lie, I am situated.

vero, *conj.*, but, indeed, however.

vert-o, -ere, -i, **vers**-um, *v.t.* 3, I
   turn.

vest-io, *v.t.* 4, I clothe.

vĕt-o, -are, -ui, -ĭtum, *v.t.* 1,
   I forbid.

vĕt-us, -ĕris, *adj.*, old.

vi-a, -ae, *f.*, a way, a road.

vicies, *adv.*, twenty times.

vĭd-eo, -ere, **vīd**-i, **vīs**-um,
   v.t. 2, I see; *pass.*, I seem.

vigil-ia, -iae, *f.*, a watch.

viginti, *num. adj. indecl.*, twenty.

vinc-ulum, -uli, *n.*, a chain,
   fetter (vincio, I bind).

vir-tus, -tūtis, *f.*, courage.

vis (*pl.*, **vir**-es, -ium), *f.*,
   strength, violence.

vis-us. *See* video.

vit-o, *v.t.* 1, I avoid.

vitr-um, -i, *n.*, woad.

viv-o, -ere, **vix**-i, **vict**-um, *v.i.*
   3, I live.

voc-o, *v.t.* 1, I call.

vol-o, **vel**-le, **volu**-i, *v. irreg.*,
   I am willing, I wish.

volupt-as, -ātis, *f.*, pleasure.

Volusēn-us, -i, *m.*, Volusenus.

vuln-us, -ĕris, *n.*, a wound.

vult-is, *from* volo.

EXERCISES

Usual order of words in a simple sentence: –
1. Subject with extensions.
2. Adverbs or other extensions of Predicate.
3. Indirect Object.
4. Direct Object.
5. Predicate.

I

RULES TO BE LEARNT

(1) A verb agrees with the subject of the sentence in **gender**, **number**, and **person**.

(2) Adjectives agree with nouns in **gender, number**, and **case**.

(3) Transitive verbs usually take an **accusative** of the object.

1. (It) is now summer.

2. Of our enemies.

3. We are setting out.

4. For all the Britons.

5. In our wars.

6. We shall supply help.

7. Our enemies determined to set out.

II

RULE.—Certain prepositions require the **accusative** case: **ante, apud, ad, circiter, contra, in** (into) **ob, per, post, praeter, prope, propter.**

1. We know the place.
2. He knew that place.
3. They are unknown to Caesar.
4. No one except you was known to me.
5. Except Caesar, no one set out.
6. The traders know the sea coast.

III

RULE.—Certain prepositions require the **ablative** case: as **ab, cum, de, ex, in** (in), **pro, sine, sub** (*rest under*).

1. He set out with the traders.
2. We shall set out in a ship.
3. He wishes to approach the island.
4. Caesar wishes to send forward his forces.
5. I have been sent forward to the island with all the ships.
6. All the ships were in the harbour.

IV

RULE.—Certain verbs require a **dative** case of the object: **adpropinquo, desum, ignosco, impero, noceo, objicio, obtempero, occurro, praesum, pareo, resisto.**

1. We shall obey the Romans.
2. The traders obeyed Caesar.

3. The hostages would have obeyed the lieutenant.
4. The inhabitants will make a fleet.
5. The ships will come to the war.
6. The lieutenant ordered me to come.

V

RULE.—A **point** of time (time *'when'*) is expressed by the **ablative** case; **duration** of time (time *'how long'*) by the **accusative**.

1. Caesar sent the ships home.
2. On that day the fleet will return.
3. The king is not faithful to the Romans.
4. His courage does not seem to be great.
5. The enemy will not dare to approach the island.

VI

1. Caesar wishes to prepare ships.
2. Caesar's plan is known to the enemy.
3. In the fifth year war was made.
4. The season of the year is not suitable for war.
5. We dare not tarry in this place.
6. Part of the enemy tarried in this place on account of the season of the year.

VII

RULE.—Write **mecum, tecum, secum, nobiscum, vobiscum, quocum, quibuscum** for cum me, cum te, etc.

1. He had with him eighty ships.

2. They held the harbour for eighteen days.
3. On the fifth day the ships were seen.
4. He tarried with me eight days.
5. On the fifth day he will return with you.
6. The ships were detained by the wind eighteen days.

VIII

RULE.—When '**him**,' '**his**,' '**them**,' '**their**,' etc., mean the same person or persons as the subject of the sentence, translate by the proper case of **se** and **suus**.

1. He sends his cavalry to the war.
2. Caesar sent his ambassador to the king.
3. Caesar ordered his soldiers to follow him (*that is,* Caesar).
4. The lieutenants had eight soldiers with them.
5. The Romans reached Britain with their ships.
6. Caesar had eighteen ships with him.
7. The Romans embarked upon their ships.

IX

RULE.—When '**him**,' '**his**,' '**them**,' '**their**,' etc., do **not** mean the same person as the subject of the sentence, but refer to someone else mentioned before, use the proper case of '**is**,' '**ea**,' '**id**.' **His** = 'of him' = **ejus**. **Their** = 'of them' = **eorum**.

1. His cavalry (*pl.*) was sent.
2. The place seems to them to be suitable.

3. Caesar assembled them.

4. Their ships have been seen.

5. The soldiers followed him (*that is*, Caesar).

6. For five days Caesar was waiting for them.

X

RULE.—Several verbs require an **ablative** case, as **utor, fungor** (I perform), **fruor** (I enjoy), **vescor** (I eat).

1. The Romans use ships in battle.

2. We shall not use the cavalry.

3. Caesar will use a suitable place for (*ad*) the battle.

4. The ships were drawn up on the shore.

5. He gave them (*dative*) the signal.

6. We do not use ships.

XI

RULE.—Transitive verbs in the passive voice take an **ablative** case to express the **instrument** (the thing *by which*).

1. The ships are held back by the waves (*fluctus, -us*).

2. The sea is shut in by the mountain.

3. The soldier hurls the javelin with his hand.

4. The weight of the armour (*arma, pl.*) impedes the soldiers.

5. The soldiers are impeded by the weight of the armour.

6. They are not accustomed to use heavy armour.

XII

RULE.—Transitive verbs in the passive voice take **a** or **ab** with the **ablative** case to express the **agent** (the person *by whom*). **A** is used before words commencing with a consonant, **ab** before words commencing with a vowel.

1. Our soldiers had been terrified by the appearance of the barbarians.
2. Our soldiers will not be terrified by the enemy (*pl.*).
3. The enemy (*pl.*) are terrified by this kind of warfare.
4. The ships are being propelled by oars.
5. The soldiers were being led (*ducere*) by Caesar.
6. The ships had been drawn up by the soldiers.
7. The signal had been given by Caesar.

XIII

RULE. – An **ablative** case may combine with a **participle** to express the **time**, **cause**, **instrument**, or **manner** of the action of the principal verb in the sentence, as **Navibus factis**, Caesar in Britanniam transiit. We usually express the same thing in English by a complete sentence beginning with 'when', 'while,' 'if,' etc. This construction is called **ablative absolute**.

1. While the soldiers were hesitating, he leaped down.
2. When the enemy had been seen, the soldiers returned to the ships.
3. If the eagle is surrendered, I shall not return.

4. If the soldiers hesitate, the eagle will be surrendered.

5. The signal having been given, the soldiers leaped down from the ship.

6. The standard-bearer will throw himself into the sea.

7. With Caesar (as) our general, we shall not fear disgrace.

XIV

RULE.—The English infinitive expresses a **purpose**, as He came *to see* the games. In Latin a purpose is expressed by **ut** (= in order that) with **pres.** or **imperf. subjunctive**, as vēnit **ut** ludos videret. The **pres. subj.** is used after the **present, fut. simple, perfect** (with '*have*'), **fut. perfect** in the principal sentence. The **imperf. subj.** is used after the **imperfect, perfect** (without '*have*'), and **pluperfect** in the principal sentence.

1. He urges his horse, that he may see the enemy.

2. He urged his horse, that he might pursue the enemy.

3. He goes out to see (*purpose*) the enemy.

4. We shall have gone out to see the place.

5. We have gone out to see the horses.

6. We are going out to see the ships.

XV

(RECAPITULATORY)

1. The enemy was seen by Caesar.

2. When the ships are filled (*abl. abs.*), we shall make an attack.

3. The horses were terrified by the attack.

4. Caesar will use the ships.

5. If the ships follow (*abl. abs.*), we shall capture the island.

6. His horses were captured.

7. Having captured the horses (*abl. abs.*), he will return.

8. Caesar followed the enemy, that he might put them to flight (*fugare*).

XVI

RULE.—Verbs meaning '**to say**,' '**to tell**,' '**to inform**,' '**to promise**,' or with any meaning implying '**speech**,' require the subject of the clause that follows to be in the **accusative case**, and the predicate in the **infinitive mood**. In English after these words we insert '**that**,' which is untranslated in Latin, as, He says that Caesar has come = Dicit Caesarem venisse.

1. He says that the enemy have sent ambassadors.

2. He promises to come [that he will come].

3. They say that the ambassadors have come.

4. Caesar promised to send [that he would send] help.

5. The ambassadors say that they were thrown into chains.

6. We promise to come [that we will come] with the ambassadors.

N.B.—Verbs of '*promising*' require a fut. infinitive and the accusative of the pronoun.

XVII

RULE.—Same as preceding exercise.

1. Caesar says that he pardons the soldiers
    [rule of Ex. iv.].
2. Caesar promises to pardon the soldiers.
3. The enemy promised to send hostages.
4. Caesar says that the Britons made war without cause.
5. He promises that he will not make war without
    cause.
6. Having sent ambassadors (*abl. abs.*), Caesar
    seeks peace.

XVIII

RULE.—A Relative Pronoun is put in the same **gender, number,** and **person** as its antecedent; but its case is determined by its use in its own sentence.

1. The ships which were approaching Britain were seen
    from the camp [Rule of Ex. iv.].
2. A storm arose, which filled the ships with water.
3. This is the island which Caesar has conquered.
4. I see the ships, which are coming into harbour.
5. The enemies, whom Caesar has subdued, are many.
6. I have seen the hostages, who were given to us.

XIX

RULE.—The **Infinitive Mood** of a verb is really a **Verbal Noun** in the neuter gender, of which the gerunds are the oblique cases; as **navigare** = sailing. Nom. and acc., **navigare**; acc. after prepositions, **navigandum**; gen., **navigandi**; dat., **navigando**; abl., **navigando**.

1. Sailing is not easy (*facil-is, -e*).
2. I love (*amare*) sailing.
3. These ships are useful (for use) for (*ad*) sailing.
4. We have come for the sake of (*causâ*) wintering.
5. I had an opportunity of sailing.
6. They came into Britain by sailing.
7. This place is useful for (*ad*) wintering.

XX
(Recapitulatory)

1. Caesar determines to come.
2. An opportunity of crossing will be given (xix.).
3. The camp, that Caesar made, was useless for wintering (xix.).
4. Caesar says that he will come after the battle (xvi.).
5. When the Britons are subdued (xiii.) we shall cross over.
6. He crosses the sea to wage war with the Britons (xiv.).

XXI

Rule.—Verbs relating to the mind or the senses may take an **accusative** with the **infinitive** after them: such verbs are **to see, to feel, to know, to hear, to think, to believe**, etc.

1. Caesar knows that the lieutenants have come.

2. I suspect that hostages will be given.

3. I think that these (things) will be useful (for use) to us.

4. Caesar thinks that the lieutenants are collecting corn.

5. Caesar thinks that corn is being collected.

6. I think that twelve ships were lost.

7. I suspect that you know all our plans.

XXII

(Recapitulatory)

1. He promises *to send* other ships (xvi.).

2. I suspect that he has sent twelve ships (xxi.).

3. The lieutenants announce that the ships have come.

4. This is the legion that Caesar sent *to forage* (use supine in -um).

5. Caesar used three legions *for foraging* (*ad* with *acc.* of gerund).

6. The enemy's design was known to Caesar.

7. Caesar orders hostages to be given to him.

8. It is announced to Caesar that three legions have been seen.

9. The general orders three legions *to set out* with him (xiv.).

10. Caesar suspected the design of the enemy from (*ex*) the dust that he saw in that direction (*pars*).

11. Their design of foraging was known to Caesar.

12. Three legions have been sent *to forage*
    (use supine in -um).

XXIII

Quum (= when) takes either **indicative** or **subjunctive**. It takes *indicative* if **simple time** is expressed; *subjunctive*, to denote **thought**; whether it be **cause** (= since), **succession** (= when), **contrast** (= 'although' or 'whereas').

1. When Caesar had ascertained this, he ordered the ambassadors to remain.
2. When they had laid down their arms, they followed the general.
3. When Caesar had come into the camp, he ordered the soldiers to reap the corn.
4. When the cavalry had surrounded the camp, the legion was thrown into confusion.
5. Caesar suspects that the enemy will come by night.
6. The general ascertains that the cavalry have laid down their arms.

XXIV

RULE.—Same as preceding exercise.

1. The noise of the wheels frightens our horses.
2. When the charioteers had leaped down from (their) chariots, they fought on foot.
3. When Caesar had ridden through (*perequitare*) the line (*acies*) he ordered the cavalry to advance (*procedere*).

4. When they see the cavalry (*simple time*), they leap down from the chariots.

5. The general rides through the line, that he may encourage (*hortari*) the soldiers.

6. When the general has been killed (*simple time*), the soldiers lay down their arms.

XXV

RULE.—'That' after '**so**,' '**such**,' '**so great**,' etc., is expressed in Latin by **ut** with the **subjunctive**; **ut** then introduces a **consequence**. The rule for the sequence of tenses is the same as in Ex. xiv.

1. So great (*tantus*) is the noise of the wheels that it frightens our horses.

2. The general is so (*tam*) skilful (*perīt-us, -a, -um*) that he conquers the enemy.

3. The place is so steep that we cannot check the horses.

4. They are so skilful that they can turn their horses in a very small space.

5. The general's horse is so swift (*incitatus*) that it is checked with difficulty (*aegre*).

6. This kind of fighting (*pugna*) is so new (*novus*) that it frightens our soldiers.

XXVI

RULE.—The **Gerundive** is a **Verbal Adjective**. In translating the English verbal noun ending in **-ing** into Latin, if the verbal comes from a transitive verb, the **gerundive** is to be used instead of the gerund, and the following substantive, instead of being in the accusative case, is drawn into the case in which the gerund would have been, if it had been used. Thus you can translate 'the hope of making booty' by *spes praedandi* (intransitive) or by *spes praedae faciendae* (transitive), but NOT by *spes faciendi praedam*.

1. The hope of engaging in battle.
2. The fear of seeing the enemy.
3. The hope of gaining liberty.
4. An opportunity of restraining the soldiers.
5. Caesar has many opportunities of coming (*gerund*).
6. Many opportunities of seeing the battle were given to us.
7. The time is suitable for (*ad*) repairing (*reficere*) the ships.
8. We have hopes of seeing the army.
9. We shall have many opportunities of making booty.

XXVII

RULE.—**Direct Questions** are asked in Latin by means of **Interrogative Pronouns** and **Adverbs**, and by the particles **num**, **nonne** and **-ne**. **Num** expects the answer 'no,' **nonne**, 'yes,' and **-ne**, which must be attached to the first word of the sentence, simply asks for information. The chief interrogative pronouns are, **quis**, who? **ecquis**, any? **qualis**, of what kind? **quantus**, how great? **quot**, how many? and the chief interrogative adverbs, **ubi**, where? **unde**, whence? **quando**, when? **cur**, why?

1. Who is able to follow?
2. Have not ambassadors been sent by Caesar? [Yes.]
3. Have you seen the general? [No.]

4. Have you not seen the cavalry? [Yes.]
5. Are you able to come?
6. How many soldiers had Caesar? Don't you know?
7. How great is the army?
8. Do you think that Caesar will depart before the winter?
9. Who can escape danger?
10. When will you come?

XXVIII

RULE.—*See preceding exercise.*

1. How great is the number of the hostages?
2. How many ships had Caesar?
3. Can they be brought to the island?
4. Do you not think that Caesar is a good (*bon-us, -a, -um*) general?
5. Do you think that the soldiers will fight without their general?
6. Has not the general set out for (*ad*) the army?

XXIX

(RECAPITULATORY)

1. Caesar tarried five days in the camp.
2. He ordered the legions to follow him.
3. What wind is blowing?
4. The time is unsuitable for (*ad*) making the harbour.
5. Ships were sent to defend the harbour.

6. Caesar sends the five legions which he had left in camp.
7. Did you not promise to come? [Yes.]
8. Have you heard (*audire*) that the general will furnish corn?
9. Have you not had many opportunities of coming?

XXX

RULE.—The **gerundive** agreeing in **gender** and **number** with the subject of a sentence may combine with any part of the verb '**esse**' to form the predicate. This construction expresses *duty, fitness,* or *necessity,* as Virtus laudanda est, = Valour is to be praised = Valour ought to be praised = Valour must be praised.

1. The soldiers must be praised.
2. The island ought to be captured.
3. The Britons must be subdued.
4. Corn must be furnished for the troops.
5. The ships must be left in the harbour.
6. The course of the ships must be changed (*mutare*).
7. Caesar is to be praised on account of his courage.

XXXI

RULE.—The gerundive takes a **dative** with it to denote the agent *by whom* instead of the ablative with *a* or *ab*.

1. The courage of the Britons is to be praised by the Romans.
2. The enemies must be subdued by us.

3. Labour must not be relaxed by us.
4. The plan of the general must be approved of by good soldiers.
5. Our ranks must not be broken by the enemy.
6. A time suitable for sailing must be sought by the general.

XXXII

REMARK.—The **Gerundive** is **passive**. It is used to translate '*must*' or '*ought*' with an active verb in English by turning the sentence first into the Passive construction and then translating literally, thus: We must praise valour = Valour is to be praised by us = Virtus nobis laudanda est. Turn the following sentences in this way before translating.

1. You must praise the soldiers.
2. Caesar must furnish corn.
3. We must see the ships.
4. We must subdue the Britons.
5. We must praise the labours of the soldiers.
6. I must leave the island.

XXXIII

RULE.—An **Indirect Question** is one that depends upon such verbs as **ask, doubt, know,** &c. **Interrogatives** introduce the indirect question (as in xxvii.), and the verb is in the **subjunctive mood**.

Rule for sequence of tenses same as in xiv.

Where are you?   (Direct Question.)   Ubi es?

I asked him where you were. (Indirect Question.) Rogavi eum ubi esses.

1. Where is the enemy? [Direct Question.]
2. I will ask [*rogare*] where the enemy is. [Indirect Question.]
3. Caesar did *not know* [*ignorare*] where the enemy was.
6. I ask you why (*cur*) you do not come.
5. I shall ascertain where Caesar is.
6. He will show me (*dat.*) where the enemy have encamped.
7. I asked the general how many legions he had.

XXXIV
(RECAPITULATORY)

1. The ships must be drawn up, and the camp must be fortified.
2. Ten days must be spent in this work.
3. How many days will you spend?
4. I will ask Caesar how many days he spent in repairing the ships. [xxxiii.]
6. How great is the army?
6. The general replied (*respondēre*) that he had four thousand men. [xvi.]
7. I asked the general how many days he had spent.
8. Did you not ascertain where the enemy had encamped? [xxvii.]
9. Caesar ascertains that the Britons have lost thirty ships. [xxi.]

XXXV (Recapitulatory)

1. When the general had seen the enemy, [xxiii.] he commanded the soldiers to draw up the ships, [xvi.] and to fortify the camp.
2. He did not think that the enemy would come. [xxi.]
3. Nevertheless [*tamen*, second word in sentence] he left one legion to guard [= for a guard to] the camp.
4. And set out by night to meet Caesar. [xiv.]
5. When he had returned, he was asked where Caesar was. [xxxiii.]
6. He replied that Caesar had not been seen.

XXXVI

Rule.—Verbs of **making**, **calling**, **thinking**, **believing**, &c., require the **Nom. Case** after them when they are in the Passive Voice: as Creatur Consul, = he is made consul: insula appelatur Mona, = the island is called Mona.

1. This island was called Britain.
2. The winter is thought to be very short.
3. A part of the legion was called a cohort.
4. One part of the year is called winter.
5. Caesar is made general.
6. He is thought to be the best general.
7. The king was called Cassivellaunus.

XXXVII (Recapitulatory)

1. The nights are shorter in Britain than in Gaul.
2. The island is thought to be Britain.

3. Is all the island inhabited? [No.]
4. Do not the inhabitants till the fields? [Yes.]
5. The Belgae crossed over that they might make booty. [xiv.]
6. The enemy will come *for the sake of* (*causâ* with gen. case) making booty. [xxvi.]
7. After making booty [xiii.] the enemy will cross over.

XXXVIII (Recapitulatory)

1. The Britons are said to use lead.
2. Is (there) not a large quantity of iron in Britain? [Yes.]
3. There is such (*tant-us, -a, -um*) a quantity of iron in Britain, that the inhabitants use it for many purposes (*ad multas res*). [xxv.]
4. Do the Britons use buildings? [No.]
5. Do you not think that Britain is milder than Gaul? [Yes.]
6. Why do you think that it is not lawful to use lead?

XXXIX (Recapitulatory)

1. Corn is to be sown in the winter. [xxx.]
2. Which is the most civilized people of Britain?
3. Have not very many men been killed in battle? [Yes.] [xxvii.]
4. How many men have you lost? [xxvii.]
5. He asked how many men we had lost. [xxxiii.]
6. He had an intention of sowing corn. [xxvi.]
7. They go out to sow corn. [xiv.]

XL

RULE.—Instead of an **adverb** with the predicate, an **adjective** agreeing with the subject expressed or understood, may sometimes be used, as *incolumes redierunt* = they returned safely.

1. The enemies show themselves in scattered bands.
2. They did this unwillingly (*invitus* = unwilling).
3. They thoughtlessly (*imprudens*) make an attack.
4. Caesar returned safely to the camp.
5. The Britons vigorously break through our cavalry.
6. The Britons thoughtlessly encamped upon the hills.

XLI

RULE.—**Causâ** (= for the sake of) with the **genitive** of the gerund of an intransitive verb, or with the **genitive** of a noun and a **genitive** of a transitive verb agreeing with it, may be used to express a **purpose**, as, Caesar *pabulandi causâ* tres legiones misit = Caesar sent three legions to forage; Caesar *hostium expellendorum causâ* legionem unam misit = Caesar sent one legion to dislodge the enemy.

1. Caesar sent five soldiers to forage.
2. They go into the fields to sow corn.
3. They go to till the fields.
4. Caesar will send soldiers to fortify the camp.
5. Caesar sent the legions into Gaul to winter.
6. Two legions were sent to make an attack.

XLII

(RECAPITULATORY)

1. Caesar orders the cavalry to cross the river.

2. An opportunity of following was not given. [xxvi.]

3. Having sent forward the cavalry, Caesar delays. [xiii.]

4. The soldiers were sent into the fields to reap the corn. [xiv.]

5. The bank was so exceedingly well fortified that the cavalry were not able to cross the river. [xxv.]

XLIII (Recapitulatory)

1. All hope of making booty was laid aside. [xxvi.]

2. Caesar had sent two legions to lay waste the fields. [xli.]

3. Having dismissed (his) forces, Caesar returned to the city. [xiii. or xxiii.]

4. The Roman soldier unwillingly gives himself to flight. [xl.]

5. Caesar unwillingly suffered the legions to leave the camp [xl.]

6. An opportunity of engaging with the enemy will be given. [xxvi.]

XLIV (See Exercise xvi)

Rule.—The **future** infinitive is used after the verbs 'to **promise**,' 'to **hope**,' 'to **undertake**,' where in English we use the present infinitive, as, He hopes to come = sperat se venturum esse.

1. He promises to send ambassadors.

2. He promised to ask Caesar.

3. They have promised to send hostages.

4. He hopes (*sperare*) to see his father.

5. They hope to avoid death by flight.

6. We hope that the king will defend the town.

XLV

RULE.—See preceding exercise.

1. Caesar promised to defend the soldiers.

2. I hope Caesar will set out before the winter.

3. The soldiers hoped that Caesar would not leave the town.

4. Caesar had promised that he would not leave the town.

5. I hope that a large number of men will assemble.

6. The legions promised to surrender themselves to the enemy.

XLVI

RULE.—When **ut** with subj. expresses a **purpose**, **ut** becomes **ne** when there is a **negative** in the sentence; when **ut** with subj. denotes a **consequence**, if there be a **negative** in the sentence, **ut** remains and the negative is expressed by **non**. Observe the following variations:

	Purpose.	*Consequence.*
(*a*) **That...not**	(1) **ne**	(2) **ut...non**.
(*b*) **That nobody**	(1) **ne quis**	(2) **ut nemo**.
(*c*) **That nothing**	(1) **ne quid**	(2) **ut nihil**.
(*d*) **That never**	(1) **ne unquam**	(2) **ut nunquam**.

1. He commands the legions not to (*a* 1) attack the camp.

2. He orders that nobody (*b* 1) may come into the camp.

3. Caesar commands the legions not to (*a* 1) take prisoners.

4. I ask you not to (*a* 1) come before night.

5. I commanded the legions not to (*c* 1) plunder anything.

6. Cassivellaunus was so greatly moved by the revolt of the citizens, that he never (*d* 2) returned to the town.

7. He had received so many losses that he was not (*a* 2) able to pay tribute.

XLVII (RECAPITULATORY)

1. Caesar orders the general to lead back [xiv.] the army.

2. The number of the soldiers is so great that the ships are not able to carry all. [xxv. and xlvi.]

3. The harbour was so small that it was not able to receive all the ships. [xxv. and xlvi.]

4. Have not the ships been repaired? [Yes.]

5. After a storm follows a calm.

6. When the soldiers had repaired the ships, they decided to sail.

VOCABULARY
(English–Latin)

The Roman Numerals refer to the Exercises;
the other Numerals to the Chapters.

able (to be), 3.
account of (on), 6.
accustomed (to be), 10.
advance (to), 8.
after, 6.
all, 1.
anything, xlvi.
ambassador, 4.
announce (to), 22.
appearance, 12.
approach (to), 13.
arise (to), 18.
armour, 11.
arms, 11.
army, 19.
ascertain (to), 2.
ask (to), xxxiii.
assemble (to), 3.
attack (an), 15.

avoid (to), 44.

bank, 42.
barbarian, 5.
battle, 10.
be (to), 1.
before, 35.
Belgae, 28.
best, 30.
blow (to), 29.
bold, xl.
booty, 26.
break (to), 19.
bring to (to), 28.
Britain, 1.
Briton, 1.
building, 27.
by, 4.

Caesar, 1.
call (to), 22.
calm, 47.
camp, 18.
can (I), 3.
capture (to), 15.
carry (to), 47.
Cassivellaunus, 35.
cause, 11.
cavalry, 10.
chain, 16.
change (to), xxx.
charioteer, 10.
check (to), 25.
citizen, 46.
civilized, 39.
cohort, 22.
collect (to), 17.
come (to), 4.
command (to), 4.
conquer, 16.
corn, 19.
courage, 5.
course, 15.
cross over (to), 20.

danger, 27.
dare (to), 5.
day, 5.
death, 44.
decide, 28.
defend (to), 29.
delay (to), 6.

depart (to), 20.
design, 4.
detain (to), 7.
determine (to), 1.
difficulty, 11.
direction, 1.
disgrace, 13.
dismiss (to), 26.
draw up (to), 5.
dust, 22.

eagle, 13.
easy, xix.
eighteen, 7.
eighty, 7.
embark (to), 8.
encamp (to), 31.
encourage (to), 9.
enemy, 1.
enagage in (to), 5.
engage with (to), 39.
escape (to), 27.
exceedingly well, 32.
except, 2.

faithful, 5.
fear, 25.
fear (to), 13.
field, 17.
fifth, 5.
fight (to), 11.
fill (to), 15.
five, 29.

fleet, 4.
flight, 15.
follow (to), 8.
foot, 12.
for, 22.
forage (to), 22.
forces, 3.
fortify, 32.
four, 43.
frighten (to), 12.
from, 4.
furnish (to), 19.

gain (to), 23.
Gaul, 19.
general, 13.
give (to), 4.
go (to), 42.
go out (to), 24.
great, 5.
greatly, 3.
guard, 7.

hand, 11.
harbour, 2.
have (to), 5.
hear (to), xxix.
heavy, 11.
help, 1.
hesitate (to), 13.
hill, 8.
him, 17.
himself, 3.

his, 3.
hold (to), 7.
hold back (to), 7.
home, 5.
hope, 43.
horse, 11.
hostage, 4.
how great, 26.
how many, 26.
hurl (to), 11.

impede (to), 11.
in, 1.
inhabit, 37.
inhabitants, 3.
intention, 4.
into, 1.
iron, 38.
island, 3.

javelin, 9.

kill (to), 23.
kind, 2.
king, 5.
know (to), 2.
know (not to), 32.

labour, 30.
large, 5.
lawful, 38.
lay aside (to), 23.
lay down (to), 23.

lay waste (to), 43.
lead, 38.
lead (to), 42.
lead back (to), 26.
leap down (to), 13.
leave (to), 6.
legion, 13.
liberty, 26.
lieutenant, 4.
line, 27.
lose (to), 19.
loss, 46.
love (to), xix.

make (to), 6.
man, 2.
many, 34.
me, 13.
meet (to), 14.
milder, 38.
mountain, 9.
move (to), 12.
move deeply (to), 12.

nevertheless, 1.
new, 22.
night, 18.
by night, 23.
nobody, xlvi.
noise, 24.
no one, 2.
not, 3.
now, 1.

number, 6.

oar, 12.
obey, 28.
on account of, 6.
one, 9.
opportunity, 6.
order (to), 4.
our, 1.

pardon (to), 17.
part, 1.
pay (to), 46.
peace, 16.
people, 39.
place, 2.
plan, 4.
plunder (to), 43.
praise (to), 30.
prepare (to), 6.
prisoner, 31.
promise (to), 5.
propel (to), 12.
provoke (to), 40.
purposes, 38.
pursue (to), 15.
put to fight (to), 15.

quantity, 3.

rank, 14.
reach (to), 8.
reap (to), 23.

receive (to), 33.
relax (to), 21.
remain (to), 22.
repair (to), 19.
reply (to), xxxiv.
restrain (to), 9.
return (to), 5.
revolt, 46.
ride through (to), 24.
river, 32.
Roman, 4.

safely, 28.
sail (to), 19.
say (to), 17.
sea, 9.
sea coast, 2.
season, 8.
see (to), 5.
seek (to), 17.
seem (to), 5.
seldom, 32.
send (to), 5.
send forward (to), 3.
set out (to), 1.
ship, 3.
shore, 9.
short, 3.
shorter, 3.
show (to), 26.
shut in (to), 9.
signal, 9.
small, 1.

so, 19.
so great, 13.
so many, 46.
soldier, 9.
sow (to), 39.
space, 25.
spend (to), 32.
standard bearer, 13.
steep, 25.
storm, 8.
subdue (to), 16.
suffer (to), 33.
suitable, 6.
summer, 1.
supply (to), 1.
surrender (to), 13.
surround (to), 23.
suspect (to), 21.
swift, 25.

take (to), 15.
tarry (to), 6.
ten, 31.
terrify (to), 12.
that (*conj.*), 13.
that (*dem.*), 2.
their, 3.
them, 17.
themselves, 3.
think (to), 36.
this, 2.
thirty, 27.
thousand, 7.

three, 29.
throw into (to), 13.
throw into confusion (to), 14.
till (to), 37.
town, 45.
trader, 2.
tribute, 46.
turn (to), 27.
twelve, 21.
two, 22.

unknown, 2.
unwillingly, xl.
upon, 1.
urge (to), 11.
us, 37.
use (to), 10.
useful (for use), 3.
useless, 19.

very many, 19.
very small, 3.

vigorously, 14.

wage (to), 6.
wait (to), 9.
war, 1.
warfare, 1.
water, 11.
wave, xi.
weight, 11.
what, 46.
wheel, 24.
when, 16.
where, 12.
which, 3.
while, 22.
who (*interrog.*), 46.
wind, 7.
winter (to), 19.
wish (to), 3.
with, 3.
without, 17.
work, 32.

year, 6.

INDEX

The Numbers refer to the Chapters.